OAK CREEK CANYON
AND THE
RED ROCK COUNTRY
OF ARIZONA

OAK CREEK CANYON
AND THE
RED ROCK COUNTRY
OF ARIZONA

A Natural History and Trail Guide

Stewart W. Aitchison

Illustrated by Pam Lungé

STILLWATER
CANYON PRESS
Flagstaff 1978

Cover photo by Lawrence F. Aitchison
All other photos by the author except as noted

Copyright© 1978 Stewart W. Aitchison

Library of Congress Catalog Card Number 78-53385

SECOND PRINTING

Printed by Classic Printers, Prescott, Arizona
United States of America

To my Parents and Ann

ACKNOWLEDGEMENTS

Without the help, advice, and expertise of many individuals, this book could never have been written. The staff of the Coconino National Forest Supervisor's Office and the Sedona Ranger District Office have been most helpful in the preparation of this book. I would also like to thank the staff members of the Museum of Northern Arizona for their input and encouragement and John Irwin of Northern Arizona University Library Special Collections and the folks of the Northern Arizona Pioneer's Historical Society for allowing the use of their historical photographs. Many private individuals gave graciously and unselfishly of their time and knowledge; notably, Dixon Fagerberg, John Hildebrand, Norman Sharber, and Bill Williams. Special thanks go out to Jan Scott and Beth Coker who patiently and carefully typed and retyped the manuscript; to Pam Lunge, who drew the excellent figures; and to my friend, Ann Kramer, who kept me from procrastinating.

Any misconceptions or errors in the text are entirely my responsibility.

Cathedral or Courthouse Rock at Red Rock Crossing

PREFACE

This book is the first in a series of natural history guides to the unique and spectacular areas of the Colorado Plateau. This particular volume deals with Oak Creek Canyon and the Red Rock Country of central Arizona. In the first section, the reader will be introduced to the region's climate, geology, archaeology, history, and ecology that blend together to produce the mystique and beauty that is the Red Rock Country. The following section invites the curious to explore the roads and trails to become more familiar with this canyon wonderland.

Oak Creek Canyon and the Red Rock Country has long been renowned for its outstanding beauty. In recent years, endeavors have been made to preserve the canyon's naturalness. The Forest Service has set aside the West Fork of Oak Creek and Casner Canyon as National Research Natural Areas. These two areas have been officially recognized as invaluable components of our national natural heritage. Currently, further studies are being conducted by the Forest Service and National Park Service to identify possible additional sites within this region.

I first became acquainted with Oak Creek Canyon when I was a small boy touring the Southwest with my folks. Later, I began working as a field biologist at the Museum of Northern Arizona in Flagstaff and was fortunate to do ecological studies in Oak Creek Canyon for the Coconino National Forest. It was during these studies that I discovered a paucity of published literature on the natural history and trails of the Red Rock Country. Volumes have been written extolling the aesthetic and scenic qualities of Oak Creek Canyon, but very little was readily available to the general public concerning the plants, the animals, the geology, and so forth. I decided to change that, and this book is the result of my efforts.

Some have accused me of revealing too much about the backcountry...that this will encourage over-use and crowding. But I believe that without education our wild and beautiful places will perish. It is my contention that if people realize what natural gifts exist in their environment, the less likely that these marvels will be paved over with apathy.

This guide represents one small attempt at dispensing information to at least some of the annual two million visitors to Oak Creek Canyon. Maybe a slightly better appreciation of this country will be cultivated and abuse of the environment will be lessened.

TABLE OF CONTENTS

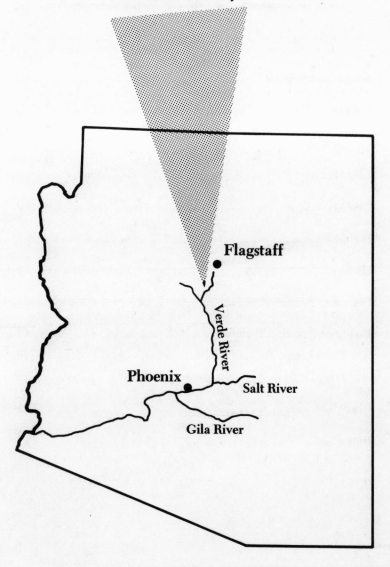

**Oak Creek Canyon
and the
Red Rock Country**

Flagstaff

Verde River

Phoenix

Salt River

Gila River

LOCATION

Oak Creek Canyon and the Red Rock Country lie along the southern escarpment of the Colorado Plateau in central Arizona. The 500 square mile area is traversed by U.S. Highway 89A and State Highway 179 and by several occasionally maintained dirt roads. Some foot or pack trails lead into the more remote sections. It is bounded on the north and east by the Mogollon Rim, a more or less continuous escarpment through central Arizona. On the southern boundary is the Verde Valley, and Sycamore Canyon Wilderness Area marks the western edge.

The area is noted for its delightful year round climate, spectacular red buttes and pine-covered plateaus, trout fishing, and camping along a verdant stream. Artist and photographers are attracted to the region; and tourists of all kinds can find lodging ranging from a wilderness setting to a plush motel-resort.

Oak Creek Canyon

CLIMATE

Climate plays an immense, although many times overlooked, role in determining the geologic, historic, and ecologic features of a particular region. For instance, the more precipitation, the faster the erosion of uplands, the quicker the accumulation of soil, the lusher the forest, and perhaps the more conducive for settlement. All the biotic and abiotic factors of our environment are interrelated, directly or indirectly; one cannot examine one specific aspect of the environment without considering the others. So let us begin with the climate of the Oak Creek area.

First we should define climate as opposed to weather. Weather is the sum total of five atmospheric or climatic elements; namely, temperature, air pressure, winds, humidity, and percipitation, for a relatively short period of time. In other words, it is the momentary state of the atmosphere. Thus we speak of the weather, not the climate, today or last week.

Climate, on the other hand, is a composite or generalization of the variety of day-to-day weather conditions. It is not just "average weather", for the variations from the mean, or average, are as important as the mean itself.

The various controls of climate are complex and intricately interwoven but the major control in the Oak Creek area is the variation in topography. Abrupt changes in elevation are dramatically marked by distinct belts of vegetation as a result of differences in temperature and precipitation. Not only elevation but the direction of exposure determines local climatic conditions; for example, generally south-facing slopes are more arid than north-facing slopes because of greater exposure to the sun.

The annual cycle of seasons follows the familiar pattern of the northern hemisphere, except that elevational differences influence the duration and intensity of each season.

Temperature: Summer temperature maxima range from 78 °F to 95 °F with minima of 45 °F to 62 °F depending on altitude. In winter the maxima range from 42 °F to 55 °F and the minima from 15 °F to 31 °F. Some examples of extremes are: Sedona Ranger Station (elevation, 4320 ft.), 108 °F in July, 1972, and 0 °F in January, 1968; Junipine (elevation, 5134 ft.), 105 °F in June, 1950, and −3 °F in January, 1949; and Flagstaff (elevation, 7006 ft.), 96 °F in June, 1970, and −22 °F in January, 1971.

On cold clear nights, which are common in winter, the cooler air will drain into the bottom of the canyons so that these areas may record the coldest temperatures. The sides of the canyons will sometimes be 5 to 10 degrees warmer than either the top or bottom. With so much uneven topography, there occur wide temperature variations from location to location. For example, although winter on the rim area almost never passes without below 0 °F temperatures, there has never been a minus temperature recorded in Sedona.

January is generally the coldest month of the year as this is when the insolation (solar radiation) is at its least concentration. On rare occasions the lowest winter temperature will occur in February but only when the January cloud cover has been high and precipitation normal. Spring temperatures show a marked rise in early March and by April average temperatures may rise to 50 °F or better. The last vestiges of cold weather leave the area below the rim by mid-April. Sedona normally does not experience temperatures below 28 °F after April 2nd and by April 15th the normal low does not go below 32 °F. Above the rim, at Flagstaff, the last 28 °F temperature occurs a full seven weeks later with the final recording of 32 °F taking place by the 8th of June.

The highest temperatures tend to come in June or July, but it is during August, with higher relative humidity, that daytime temperatures seem more unbearable. Cold weather will arrive before the end of September and readings of 32 °F will come by the end of September in the higher elevations. In the Sedona area, freezing temperatures usually do not arrive until the beginning of November.

Precipitation: Generally total annual precipitation amounts increase as one moves northeasterly from Sedona to the Mogollon Rim and from low elevations to higher elevations. Sedona Ranger Station receives about 17″ of precipitation per year; Junipine, 26″; and the Mogollon Rim, nearly 30″.

Seasonally, precipitation comes during winter and summer.

Spring and autumn tend to be periods of drought, with the spring dry spell usually lasting longer than the autumn. Even though spring tends to be the driest time of year, on the average, there is only one day less with measurable rainfall in April than in January.

Winter precipitation results from cyclonic (low pressure) storms that are brought into the area by westerly winds. These storms usually bring heavy cloud cover and strong winds from the west and northwest but not much precipitation. Occasionally, about one in every five years, a storm will be pushed farther south and the center of the low will pass over the area bringing heavier precipitation such as the storm of December, 1967, which left three feet of snow in Sedona and over seven feet along the Mogollon Rim.

The moisture-bearing storms usually arrive in the last ten days of November. Usually these cyclonic storm cycles will peak in late January and by mid-March will have been displaced north again.

Summer precipitation is derived from a completely different source. With the migration of the westerlies northward, air moves into Arizona from the clockwise circulation around an anticyclone (or high pressure cell) in the central and eastern United States. This air transports much moisture from the Gulf of Mexico. A substantial amount of the moisture is lost to the east of Coconino and Yavapai Counties, but there is enough left to cause summer to be the wettest time of the year.

Normally the summer rains commence during the second ten-day period of July and last until mid-September. These rains usually come in the form of short, late-afternoon thunderstorms, rarely lasting an hour. They can be of the cloudburst type known locally as a gully-washer, but typically are light to moderate showers bringing less than .25 inches of rainfall. The showers also tend to be very local; sometimes a person can stand half in rain and half in sunshine. The showers are usually concentrated over areas of more rugged terrain such as the canyons. The causative factors are the unequal thermal heating of the air and the orographic uplift, both resulting from the uneven topography.

About one year in seven, tropical cyclonic storms will push northward into Arizona from the Gulf of California in late

August and September, causing heavy rainfall. Such a storm struck Labor Day weekend in 1970. Five and one half inches of precipitation fell in 24 hours and 23 people were killed in Arizona due to flooding. Usually these wet autumns coincide with wet winters.

Winds: Winds are a common phenomenon of the Oak Creek Canyon area. From February through September the prevailing winds blow up the Verde Valley and then up Oak Creek and other canyons. Once in the canyons, the air is compressed and its velocity increases; this is called the venturi effect.

Late September and October bring a marked change in overall wind direction as the cyclonic westerlies are moving farther southward. Wind direction is from the north in October then moves to a more easterly direction so that by December and January the prevailing direction is northeast.

Uneven topography makes for many changes in local wind directions. Another terrain-related wind phenomenon is the daily up-canyon and down-canyon wind. During the day, intense heating results in a strong rising of air along the canyon walls. Differential heating at the head and mouth of the canyon results in an up-canyon wind. At night the process is reversed as cooler air descends the canyon. Weather can be greatly influenced by these local winds.

During the summer, dust devils are occasionally encountered. These miniature tornado-like winds generally are more of a nuisance than a hazard. These whirlwinds are formed on still, hot days when the ground is heated approximately 150 to 160 degrees Fahrenheit. As this hot surface warms the air in immediate contact with it, a potentially unstable situation is created, with very warm air underlying much cooler air. Since this air cannot turn over as an intact sheet, small thermal cells develop where upward convection is concentrated. Any wind in the vicinity of these cells gives them an angular momentum which is intensified by upward convection into the familiar rotating dust devil. Rotation of the dust devil vortex may be either clockwise or counterclockwise. Most dust devils are small and have lifespans of only two or three minutes; some, however, become quite large and can do structural damage to obstacles in their path.

Of rare occurrence in the Red Rock Country are dust

storms, sometimes called haboobs which is the past tense of the Arabic verb *hebbe*, meaning "to blow". Dust storms form when rain first begins to fall from huge cumulonimbus clouds (thunderhead type). The Pima Indians have a legend that "the rain is blind and always has to be led by the sandstorm". This initial precipitation generally evaporates before it reaches the ground. This type of rain is called a virga shower. Air cooled by the evaporating rain moves rapidly downward to the ground, where it first churns up the dust. Dense columns of dust swirl upward and merge to form a billowing wall of sand. As the cold air pushes ahead, this undercutting wedge of dense air lifts the lighter, warmer air of the desert surface and feeds it into the convective updrafts of the following cumulus cloud system to continually regenerate itself. The result is often a brief storm of considerable intensity.

FURTHER READING

Idso, Sherwood B. 1974. *Tornado or dust devil: the enigma of desert whirlwinds.* American Scientist 62(5) :530-541.

Idso, Sherwood B. 1974. *Summer winds drive dust storms across the desert.* Smithsonian 5(9) :68-73.

Pape, Bruce M.C. 1969. *Climatic Study of Coconino County, Arizona.* Master's Thesis, Arizona State University. 75 pp.

Sellers, William D. and Richard H. Hill. 1974. *Arizona Climate 1931-1972.* University of Arizona Press, Tucson. 616 pp.

Trewartha, Glenn T. 1954. *An Introduction to Climate.* Mcgraw-Hill Book Co., Inc. New York. 395 pp.

U. S. Department of Commerce. 1971. *Arizona Floods of September 5 and 6, 1970.* Natural Disaster Survey Report 70-2. 39 pp.

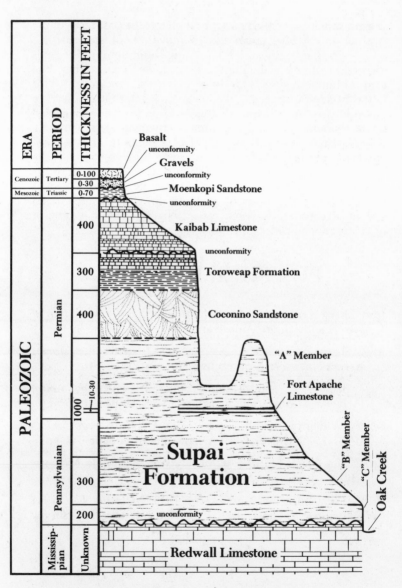

Geologic Cross-Section of Oak Creek Canyon

GEOLOGY

Closely tied to climate is the geology of the area. The rocks, the soils, the varied topography not only reflect, in part, the present climatic conditions but also provide clues to past environments. Let us begin with a broad overview of the "lay of the land".

Picture the Colorado Plateau as a huge layer cake averaging 5000 feet above sea level and covering some 150,000 square miles. Across its top are a myriad of cracks and gashes revealing, in general, a thick series of horizontal beds of various kinds of sedimentary rocks. Over parts of the plateau is an "icing" of lava. Oak Creek Canyon and the Red Rock Country lie on the southern edge of this geologic layer cake.

Upon closer examination, we see that Oak Creek Canyon is 12 miles long and merges into the northeastern margin of the broad Verde River Valley. Oak Creek Canyon, at its upper end, is about 1500 feet deep and, at the lower end, near Sedona, it approaches 2500 feet in depth. The width from rim to rim averages nearly a mile.

Layers of various colored and textured rock are evident. Near Sedona, we first see red sandstones near the creek; these are overlaid by buff sandstones, then a yellowish sandstone, followed by a white limestone, and finally capped by dark gray or black lavas on the rim. The remainder of the Red Rock Country is composed of these same layers of rock, although thickness of each type may vary from place to place.

By studying each succeeding layer in detail we can learn how these particular rocks came to be there and finally how the present-day scenery was created. This branch of study is called stratigraphy.

The oldest rocks are deeply buried under the present surface, which makes them obviously difficult to study, so we shall begin with the oldest rocks exposed in the Red Rock Country. Near Indian Gardens, about 4 miles north of Sedona, at stream level, is a 200 foot cliff of light gray, fine to coarsely crystalline, pure limestone. Marine fossils such as corals and brachiopods are common, with crinoid stems ("sea lilies") being abundant.

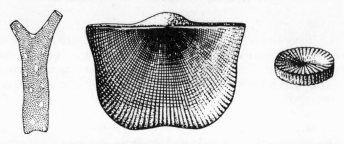

Fossil Coral   **Fossil Brachiopod**   **Fossil Crinoid Stem**

This formation, or layer, has been named the Redwall Limestone. Redwall may seem an unappropriate name for this gray rock but it was in the Grand Canyon where this layer was first studied and named. In the Grand Canyon the Redwall Limestone has been stained red on its exposed surfaces by iron oxides leached out of overlying rocks.

The presence of the marine fossils and radiometric dating suggests a sea covering this part of Arizona 300 to 340 million year ago, a period of time geologists have named the Mississippian. The purity of the Redwall Limestone suggests that streams and rivers rich in dissolved calcium carbonates derived from onshore limestone formations emptied into the Redwall Sea. The calcium carbonate precipitated out on the ocean floor along with the shells of billions of microscopic sea animals and slowly built up layer upon minute layer to form the massive formation. It is known from studying other localities, and presumably true for the Red Rock Country, that the Redwall was exposed to erosion for some length of time and then re-submerged under a sea.

Resting on the uneven surface of the Redwall and forming the spectacular red buttes and mesas of the Sedona area is the Supai Formation, named after the Havasupai Indians who live in the Grand Canyon. In the Red Rock Country, the Supai is composed of three fairly distinct units called "A", "B", and "C". The lowest member, "C", is predominantly a pale red or pink siltstone or very fine-grained sandstone. It forms ledges which are well exposed in a small "inner gorge" in the vicinity of Midgely Bridge. The middle or "B" member is a reddish-brown, fine-grained sandstone which weathers to a debris-covered slope through which occasional small ledges crop out. The upper or "A" member is a grayish orange or pale reddish brown, fine to very fine-grained sandstone. It forms the debris-free, rounded cliffs and pinnacles, such as the "Mitten" in the southern end of the canyon. It often displays a large scale honeycomb-type of weathered surface. In about the middle of the "A" member is the Fort Apache Limestone. This probably represents a relatively short period of time in which a sea from the southeast encroached upon the area depositing a 10 to 30 foot thick limestone layer. Since it is more resistant to erosion than the softer sandstone, it sometimes forms ledges (such as "Merry-go-round" on Schnebly Hill Road - see Road Log #3).

The Supai Formation is about 1500 feet thick of which about 1000 feet is "A", 300 feet is "B", and 200 feet is "C". The red iron-oxide stain suggests that these are delta or flood-plain deposits where iron minerals could readily mix with abundant oxygen. The subtle facies (rock type) changes from siltstone to sandstone indicate that the Supai sea was retreating (with the exception of the relatively brief ingression of the Fort Apache Sea). By Permian time the marine regression was in full swing. This area had become part of a vast desert. Huge sand dunes covered the landscape. Today the wind-blown dunes are preserved as the Coconino Sandstone Formation which lies on top of the Supai. In the buff-colored, cliff-forming Coconino Formation, one can see the sloping layers of these dunes where they form peculiar wedge-shaped patterns called cross-bedding. Fossilized reptile tracks are found in this formation but are almost always going uphill. For a long time scientists were puzzled why no downhill tracks could be found. Many wild and ingenious theories were developed including one that suggested that these ancient reptiles walked to the top of a dune and then were able to fly or glide to the bottom. An experiment with a present-day lizard solved the mystery. It was found that as the animal walked uphill, it left the typical distinct uphill tracks. As the lizard walked down the dune, the downward momentum of the animal produced "blurred" tracks which

Cross-bedding of the Coconino Sandstone

became further filled with sand as the animal continued down the slope.

Above the 400 foot thick Coconino is another cross-bedded sandstone, the Toroweap. Here, though, the layers are uniformly sloping within a series of horizontal beds. This type of cross-bedding is attributed to deposition in water. A sea was once again covering the area.

The Toroweap forms a very pale orange cliff some 300 feet thick. There is usually a distinct topographic break between the Coconino Sandstone and the Toroweap Sandstone in the form of a small bench. In some locations the boundary between the two is further distinguishable because of the change in appearance of the type of cross-bedding. In other places the Coconino seems to blend into the Toroweap, suggesting continuous deposition.

A slight but noticeable unconformity (an erosional surface) is found between the top of the Toroweap and the bottom of the next formation, the Kaibab Limestone. This means that the Toroweap Sea probably retreated for some length of time. The sea eventually returned and the Kaibab Limestone was deposited.

The Kaibab contains many fossils; brachiopods and sponges are very common. This formation in Oak Creek is about 400 feet thick. This is not the total original thickness, however, because the layer has been beveled by erosion.

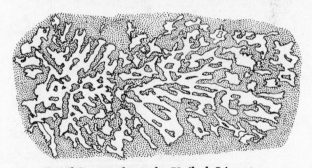

Fossil Sponge from the Kaibab Limestone

The regression of the Kaibab Sea marks the end of the Permian Age. The Triassic Period began with an interval of

Successive Basaltic Lava Flows — above Indian Gardens

erosion. Streams draining from the north and east carried in great loads of brown and red-brown sand and silt. These sediments now constitute the Moenkopi Formation. Only patches of Moenkopi remain as a result of erosion in Miocene and Pliocene times. About a 70 foot thick section is found on East Pocket Knob. Other thin remnants have been found on the east wall of Oak Creek Canyon and along the terrace block at and south of Fry Canyon. Here ripple marks (fossilized undulations produced by currents of water) typical of the formation have been found.

Fifteen million years ago during Pliocene times there was an uplift to the southwest of the Oak Creek Canyon area. As these mountains were eroded down, the gravels derived from this erosion were carried by streams to the northeast. Remnants of these gravels can be seen east of Manzanita Campground and along Schnebly Hill Road.

After another 10 million years of erosion, molten lavas came up through cracks in the ground and spread out over the surface, where they cooled to form basalt. In places seven or more successive flows piled up, one on top of another, as seen on the east wall above Banjo Bill Camp. Vertical cracks filled with lava (dikes) that lead up to some of these flows are visible along the highway near Junipine. The lava also formed massive, six-sided, vertical columns up to thirty feet in height. These columns are the result of contraction during cooling. Good examples are exposed in the lava flow facing the highway near the head of Oak Creek Canyon. Also in this area red bands may be seen between some of the lava flows. It is believed that these bands are soils baked by the hot basalt flowing over them.

Three million years ago, lava poured out of Squaw Peak (to the south of Red Rock Country) and dammed up the Verde River to form a large lake. Dissolved minerals that were coming into the lake were slowly deposited as the lake became smaller due to evaporation and as the lava dam was eroded away, allowing drainage of the lake. These deposits, termed evaporites, are the white hills and benches in the Verde Valley on the edge of the Red Rock Country. Some of the hills are gypsum, some are salt, most are mixtures of these and fresh water limestone and shales. These deposits are collectively called the Verde

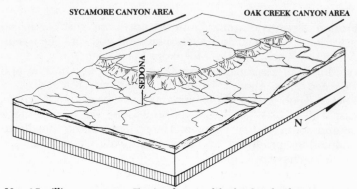

63 to 17 million years ago — Erosion due to uplift of Colorado Plateau

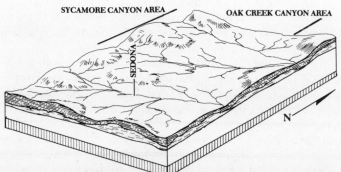

15 million years — Mountains uplift to southwest and gravels are deposited.

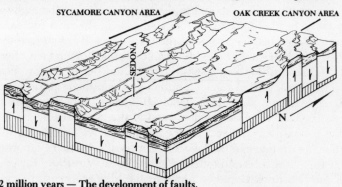

12 million years — The development of faults.

Geologic Development of the Red Rock Country

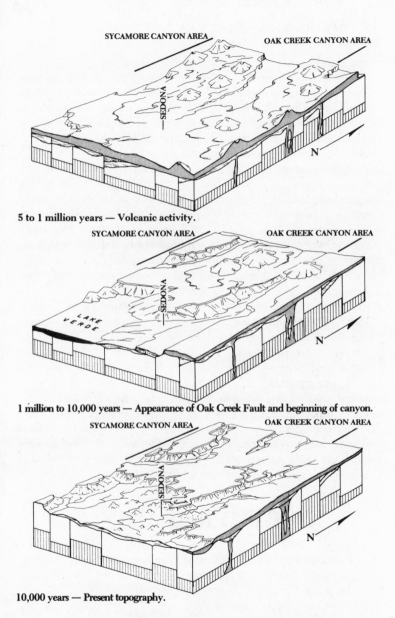

5 to 1 million years — Volcanic activity.

1 million to 10,000 years — Appearance of Oak Creek Fault and beginning of canyon.

10,000 years — Present topography.

Geologic Development of the Red Rock Country

Limestone.

Relatively recently, in the neighborhood of one million years ago, and probably while the area was gradually being raised into a high plateau, long breaks or faults developed in the rocks. The largest of these appears to have determined in considerable measure the orientation of Oak Creek Canyon, for the higher west wall is a direct result of vertical movement of approximately 500 feet along a fault that extends down the canyon. From the canyon head at the observation point, this fault is especially conspicuous. Other smaller faults, some cutting across the canyon, determine side-canyon placement. Other cracks called joints also developed. These differ from faults in that there is no relative movement of the rock involved. Joints tend to form at right angles to one another and it is along these lines of weakened rock that erosion acts fastest. The zigzagging West Fork of Oak Creek is a good example of a tributary whose orientation was predetermined by joints. Where joint systems have not developed, canyons are straighter. Mund's Canyon exemplifies this type.

The form and size of Oak Creek Canyon, and the mesas, buttes, and promontories that have been sculptured from its walls, are primarily the result of erosion. Many factors have contributed to this process. Flashfloods from cloudbursts are largely responsible for the erosion of the canyons. The processes of weathering such as frost wedging and wind and the action of plant root growth gradually widen the canyons. Steep grades and high cliffs permit gravity to speed the debris along and constantly expose new surfaces to disintegration.

FURTHER READING

Karlstrom, Thor N. V., Gordon A. Swann, and Raymond L. Eastwood. 1974. *Geology of Northern Arizona. Part II.* Geology Society of America, Rocky Mountain Section Meeting, Flagstaff, Arizona. p. 408-805.

McKee, Edwin D. 1931. *Ancient Landscapes of the Grand Canyon Region.* Northland Press, Flagstaff. 52 pp.

McKee, Edwin D. 1945. *Oak Creek Canyon.* Plateau 18(2) :25-32.

Mears, Brainerd, Jr. 1949. *Cenozoic Faults, Gravels, and Volcanics of Oak Creek Canyon, Arizona.* Unpublished Ph.D. dissertation, Columbia University 84 pp.

Mears, Brainerd, Jr. 1950. *Faulting in Oak Creek Canyon and discussion of contrary bending.* Plateau 23(2) :26-31.

Rahm, David A. 1974. *Reading the Rocks.* Sierra Club, San Francisco. 160 pp.

Shelton, John S. 1966. *Geology Illustrated.* W. H. Freeman and Co., San Francisco and London. 434 pp.

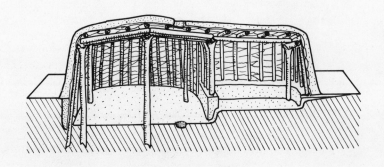

Hohokam Pithouse

PREHISTORY

Very little specific archaeological data exists for Oak Creek Canyon and the Red Rock Country. Therefore, information for this chapter was gathered and synthesized from excavations primarily on the periphery of our area, namely the Verde Valley, where Tuzigoot and Montezuma Castle National Monuments are found, Hidden House in Sycamore Canyon, Honanki and Palatki in the Red Rock Country, and work down in the Flagstaff area. As more archaeological research is undertaken in this area, the story of the prehistoric peoples will be revised and refined.

Only meager evidence of Indian occupation of the Oak Creek-Red Rock Country prior to A.D. 700 exists. In the Dry Creek area, west of Sedona, a few stone tools have been found that may date back 4000 years. (Some archaeologists believe that this quarry site may have been in use up to historical times by succeeding Indian cultures.) These tools were probably left by a nomadic hunting and gathering people, but who they were and where they came from is lost in antiquity. Charred bones indicate that they hunted deer, antelope, jackrabbits, and porcupine. They probably gathered pinyon nuts, roots, agave, grasses, cactus fruit, mesquite beans, and acorns for food.

About A.D. 700, a group of people, now called the Hohokam (a Pima word for "those who have vanished") traveled up along the Verde and/or Agua Fria Rivers from the Gila-Salt Basin. They settled along the Verde River and its tributaries in clusters of one-room pole and brush huts built partially underground, which today are called pithouses. The Hohokam built extensive irrigation ditches and planted fields of maize, beans, squash, and cotton. They made baskets and pottery. Their pottery consisted of plain brown ware for storage and cooking and buff-colored ware decorated with red designs for ceremonial use. Pieces of pottery, called sherds, are occasionally found on the surface. [Please do not collect or disturb any Indian artifacts; they are protected under State and Federal Law. Report all finds to the Museum of Northern Arizona, the Forest Service, or the National Park Service.]

By the eighth century A.D., another people (called the Sinagua, Spanish for "without water") were living above the Mogollon Rim in the Flagstaff area. They, too, lived in pithouses but practiced dry farming; that is, they depended on naturally occurring soil moisture and rainfall. The typical Sinagua pottery was a plain brown or brick-red ware.

Between A.D. 1064-1065 Sunset Crater, northeast of Flagstaff, erupted, spewing forth cinders and lava ash that eventually formed a rich mulch. (Note: some scientists put the eruption date at A.D. 1066-1067.) This factor combined with a moist period from about A.D. 1050 to 1100 greatly improved dry farming. Some of the Hohokam moved north to trade with the Sinagua people and possibly to take advantage of this new fertile farmland. Some stone dwellings were built at this time. However, by A.D. 1125, Sinagua were moving south into the Verde Valley. Perhaps it was overpopulation, climatic changes, and declining food production on the rim that triggered this move. Once in the valley, the Sinagua built small communal dwellings (called pueblos) of stone. They continued to practice dry farming on the terraces. The common small dwellings and granaries tucked away in the more remote canyons belong to this period.

Sinaqua Pueblo — Early Stage Dwelling

There was an apparent blending of Sinagua and Hohokam cultures and by A.D. 1250, large dwellings were being built on hilltops (Tuzigoot) and in large recesses of cliffs (Montezuma Castle). Between A.D. 1276 and 1299, a prolonged drought prohibited dry farming and dependence upon irrigation increased. The pueblos continued to grow.

Between A.D. 1300 and 1400, the Sinagua completely abandoned the uplands and complete river valley occupation occurred.

Montezuma Castle — Late Stage Dwelling. Photo cir. 1903

By the mid-1400's, the pueblo dwellers had abandoned the valley. Why? No one knows for sure. Perhaps overcrowding, deterioration of farmland, disease, or conflict, or a combination of these and other reasons were the cause. Where did they go? Some may have moved north and been incorporated by the Hopi. Some may have moved south into the Salt River Valley. Others may have simply abandoned the agrarian way of life and concentrated on a hunting and gathering type of subsistence, possibly becoming the forerunners of the Northeastern Yavapai.

By A.D. 1582 the Northeastern Yavapai had entered the Verde Valley. Sometime between 1400 and 1700, the Tonto Apache also moved into the area. Intermarriage between these people has led to much confusion in terminology among the non-native Americans who have dealt with these people. They have been called everything from Yavapai-Apache to Mohave to Yumans.

FURTHER READING

Martin, Paul S. and Fred Plog. 1973. *The Archaeology of Arizona.* Doubleday/Natural History Press, Garden City, N.Y. 422 pp.

McGregor, John C. 1974. *Southwestern Archaeology.* University of Illinois Press, Urbana. 511 pp.

Wormington, H.M. 1966. *Prehistoric Indians of the Southwest.* Popular Series #7. Denver Museum of Natural History, Denver, Colorado. 191 pp.

HISTORY

In May of 1583, Spanish explorer Antonio de Espejo entered the Verde Valley, probably following an old Indian trail that came down Beaver Creek (20 miles southeast of Oak Creek). Here he found Indians with "crowns of painted sticks on their heads, and jicarras of mescal and pinyon nuts and bread made from it." These were probably Yavapai Indians. Espejo's mission was primarily to locate and rescue two friars, but the Spaniards were really more interested in prospecting. They had been told of mines south and west of the Hopi mesas, but were disappointed to find they were copper mines and not silver. (Much later, in 1876, this ore deposit was to become the fabulous United Verde and Verde Extension mines, but that is another story.)

Again, in 1598, the Spanish visited the mines. This expedition was headed by Marcos Farfan de los Godos. His route approximated Espejo's, so he too only saw the Red Rock Country from a distance. The Indians Farfan found wore small wooden crosses on their heads and therefore he called them Cruzados ("people with crosses").

These Indians called themselves Wipukupa ("people at foot of the rocks or mountains"). They lived in caves or built crude pole and brush huts called wickiups. The Wipukupa planted maize in moist areas in Oak Creek, one popular spot still being called Indian Gardens.

In the early 1800's, the first American pioneers entered the Verde Valley region. These were probably trappers or prospectors who generally did not stay very long. Then began settlement by farmers and ranchers.

Indian-American pioneer relations were good until the 1850's. By then the Yavapai-Apache subsistence pattern of hunting and gathering was being threatened by the encroachment of too many settlers. It became evident to the Indians that stealing cattle and crops was by far easier if not downright necessary to continue survival. During the 1860's, open raiding was common, and by 1865 pioneer life focused around a stone fortress built out of the crumbling walls of an ancient Sinagua ruin on West Clear Creek, 25 miles south of present-day Sedona. In August of that year, First Lieutenant Antonio Abeytia and 18 foot soldiers were dispatched from Fort Whipple in Prescott to quell the raiding.

Abeytia and his men held their own in skirmishes with the Indians. The soldiers' supplies were continually critically short, so after a battle the soldiers would gather up as much of the Indians' food as possible and bring it back to camp.

In December, 1865, the soldiers' camp became officially Camp Lincoln but was changed three years later to Camp Verde to avoid confusion with the multitude of forts being honored by the late president's name. Malaria was a major concern and perhaps more soldiers and settlers were lost to this mosquito-carried menace than to Indian-inflicted wounds.

By 1870, a system of Indian reservations was being planned for the Arizona Territory, and in 1871, the Camp Verde Reservation was established for the Yavapai-Apaches living in the Verde Valley area. Also at this time, Camp Verde was moved to one-half mile south from the junction of Beaver Creek and Verde River. This is its present location; and it has been designated a State Park.

Renegades, notably Delshay and Chalipun, caused disruption of reservation life and most of the Yavapai-Apache returned to raiding the settlers. In July of 1871, the great Indian fighter General George Crook arrived from Tucson. Crook was over six feet tall, had flaming "burnside" whiskers, and usually dressed unconventionally in canvas hunting clothes. He also allowed his men a similar casual dress.

Crook apparently knew just how to subdue Indians. In November of 1872, he began his offensive. His tactic was to keep the hostiles moving, to wear them out and exhaust their food supply. Six months later, in April, Chalipun and Delshay surrendered.

Crook was equally effective in convincing the Yavapai-Apache that reservation life could not only be tolerated but profitable through the sale of surplus crops. But some ambitious ranchers and influential government officials succeeded in having the reservation abolished and having the land opened to non-Indian settlement.

About 1400 Indians were forced to march to the San Carlos

Gen. George Crook

General George Crook

reservation in east-central Arizona during the winter of 1875. Nearly 100 died enroute. Not until the 1890's did some of the Yavapai-Apache receive permission to return to the Verde Valley region. It was still another twenty years before an official reservation would be set up for their exclusive use.

Back in the Red Rock Country proper, John Jim Thompson became the first permanent settler within Oak Creek Canyon in 1876. The same year, the Beaver Head Stage Station was built 12 miles south of present-day Sedona near Dry Beaver Creek. This station was located on the old road between Albuquerque and Prescott.

The decade of 1870 to 1880 saw many people entering the Red Rock Country to homestead. It was during this time that many of the buttes and pinnacles received their names. The U.S. Department of the Interior's 1879 map of the Territory of Arizona shows the stream as "Live Oak Creek."

About 1880 C. J. "Bear" Howard built a cabin at the mouth of the West Fork of Oak Creek. Through the years the cabin was added onto by succeeding owners until today it is the famous Mayhew's Lodge, where presidents, movie stars, and writers have found hospitality and relaxation. In 1969, the lodge was

C.J. "Bear" Howard (center) — about 1890

purchased by the U.S. Forest Service which hopes to turn it into a visitor information center. It is presently a designated National Historic Site.

During the 1880's, the officers of Camp Verde had a summer camp (Camp Garden) about where the present-day junction of highways 89A and 179 is located.

Even as early as the mid-1890's, people were being attracted to the area for its beauty. Archaeologist Jesse W. Fewkes predicted in 1895 that the Red Rock Country would become very popular with tourists.

In 1901, Ellsworth Schnebly wrote his brother T. C. and his wife, Sedona, that 80 acres were for sale on the banks of Oak Creek. T. C. and his family arrive from Missouri and located a house just south of the present-day Forest Service Ranger Station. In 1902, he applied for a post office permit, submitting Oak Creek Station as the name. It was rejected because the name was too long. Finally the decision was made to call the post office Sedona.

Courtesy of Northern Arizona University Library, Special Collections

T.C. and Sedona Schnebly — 1897

In 1902 the Schnebly Hill Road was completed, shortening the trip to Flagstaff from three or four days to two days. Sedona then became the half-way station for travel between Flagstaff and Jerome, the famous copper-mining town. People continued to move into the area. In 1914, the first road through Oak

Creek Canyon to Flagstaff was finished. It crossed the creek sixteen times.

By 1922 Hollywood had discovered the Red Rock Country. The film version of Zane Grey's novel "Call of the Canyon" was filmed near West Fork, the actual setting of Grey's story. By 1959, an average of two films per year were being made in Oak Creek Canyon-Red Rock Country. These films no doubt helped publicize the area and tourism boomed. Today (1978) over two million visitors per year pass through Oak Creek Canyon.

FURTHER READING

Arizona Highways Magazine. 1959. Sedona-Oak Creek Country Issue Vol. XXXV, No. 5, May.

Arizona Highways Magazine. 1965. Oak Creek-Sedona Revisited Issue. Vol. XLII, No. 6, June.

Bartlett, Katherine. 1942. *Notes upon the routes of Espejo and Farfan to the mines in the sixteenth century. In* New Mexico Historical Review. Vol. XVII, No. l. pp 21-36.

Gifford, E. W. 1936. *Northeastern and Western Yavapai.* Univ. of California Publications Am. Arch. and Ethnology. Vol. 34, No. 4. pp. 247-354.

Schroeder, Albert H. 1959. *A study of Yavapai History; in three parts.* National Park Service, Santa Fe. 439 pp.

Sedona Westerners. 1975. *Those Early Days...Oldtimers' Memoirs.* The Verde Independent-The Sedona Westerners. 270 pp.

FLORA AND FAUNA

The Oak Creek Canyon region offers the rare opportunity to study a variety of plant and animal communities within a relatively small area. The changes in elevation, orientation of slopes, changes in rock or soil types, coupled with differences in climate from canyon bottom to canyon rim and through time, all play an integral part in determining what plants and animals can live in any one particular locale.

Within the Oak Creek Canyon-Red Rock Country are a series of plant communities ranging from comparatively moist ponderosa pine forest, with some white fir and Douglas fir, to the edge of arid desert, with representative species of ocotillo, prickly pear, and snakeweed. Eight major plant communities are recognized in our area: namely, Ponderosa Pine-Fir Forest, Chaparral, Pinyon-Juniper Woodland, Evergreen Oak Woodland, Arizona Cypress Woodland, Upper Riparian, Lower Riparian, and Desert-Grassland. There also exist numerous plant communities that cover smaller areas and are less conspicuous.

One example is the Bigtooth Maple Community found in some of the steep drainages in cooler and moister parts of Oak Creek Canyon. Additionally, there are usually not sharp dividing lines between communities but rather a gradual intergradation called an ecotone. In some localities, such as Sterling Canyon, as many as four major communities and several lesser communities may combine to form an ecotone of incredible variety. Over 600 species of vascular plants are known from the Oak Creek Canyon-Red Rock Country area.

Ponderosa Pine-Fir Forest: Along the rims of the main canyons, the dominant species is the ponderosa pine. This marks the southern edge of the largest ponderosa pine forest in the world. In protected areas where moisture and cooler air may collect, Douglas fir, white fir, an occasional Engelmann spruce, alpine fir, and a few stands of quaking aspen occur. Occasionally there is an understory of Gambel's oak, mountain mahogany, New Mexico locust, and bracken fern. This forest community

Ponderosa Pine - Fir Forest

extends down into the heads of some of the canyons. In Oak Creek Canyon this community is discontinuous downstream to just south of Bootlegger Campground, where it finally is completely replaced by more xerophytic ("dry-loving") species.

Chaparral: The chaparral community occupies slopes intermediate in aridity and temperature between forests and deserts. In Oak Creek Canyon this vegetation type extends from the southern facing canyon walls just above Pine Flats Campground and continues past Sedona, forming the largest vegetational association of the canyon.

These hot, dry areas are characterized by dense shrubs and stunted trees and are occasionally transected by pine and oak along moist clefts, especially on north facing slopes. The dominant plants are silk-tassel bush and manzanita. These form almost pure stands on some slopes, while mountain mahogany, catclaw acacia, buckbrush, and shrub live oak cover generally slightly cooler slopes.

Intrusions of many species of evergreen oaks, as well as singleleaf ash, ponderosa pine, and Arizona walnut follow the side gullies, while fernbush, rock spiraea, alligator-bark and one-seed juniper, narrowleaf and banana yucca and pinyon pine may be found on rock outcroppings. The chaparral thins considerably southward and becomes the understory of the Pinyon-Juniper, Evergreen Oak, and Arizona Cypress Communities.

Pinyon-Juniper Woodland: The Pinyon-Juniper Woodland is sometimes called the pygmy forest because of the small stature of these trees. In terms of coverage, this community is one of the most widespread in Northern Arizona. In the Red Rock Country, it is quite common especially in areas adjacent to but slightly drier than where ponderosa pine will grow.

The Pinyon-Juniper Woodland, dominated by pinyon pine and one-seed juniper (sometimes incorrectly called cedar), usually exhibits patches of the chaparral species in more open areas. Both this woodland and chaparral are intermediate between forests and deserts in terms of moisture and temperature requirements. The chaparral seems to be dominant in areas of well-drained, arid, rocky soils. On the other hand, the pinyon and juniper prefer slightly wetter and finer soils. Probably the

Chaparral

heavy chaparral understory in many places of this woodland is due to a long history of fire suppression by ranchers and the Forest Service. Arizona white oak, gray oak, and Emory oak are sparsely represented in some parts of this community.

Evergreen Oak Woodland: Within the canyons on dry benches (flat areas above the canyon bottom), the floral composition shifts to an Evergreen Oak Woodland. This complex community, often composed of dense stands of several species of oak and juniper, is typified by Gambel's oak (ironically the only deciduous oak in this community), wavyleaf oak, and one-seed juniper. Regularly scattered throughout these oak areas are clusters of netleaf hackberry, hoptree, pinyon pine, Arizona white oak, Emory oak, and Arizona cypress. Palmer oak and shrub live oak combine with graythorn, buckthorn, and other typical chaparral species to form a thick undergrowth. Many of these oaks interbreed, producing hybrids that show intermediate characteristics of the parent plants. Excellent examples of this community may be seen on the lower slopes of the east wall above Manzanita Campground, and again to the west just above the Encinoso Picnic Area.

Arizona Cypress Woodland: At the mouth of many of the Red Rock Country canyons is an unusual vegetative community composed of Arizona cypress. Arizona cypress occurs more commonly in the mountains in southern Arizona. These restricted northern woodlands are said to be relictual, meaning that sometime in the past, cypress probably covered larger areas but due to some kind of environmental change only small, isolated pockets remain.

Mountain mahogany, deerbrush, shrub live oak, buckbrush, and barberry make up the understory, although in some thick stands of cypress nearly all ground cover is shaded out. Occasional clusters of cacti, agave, and yuccas dot the more rugged, rocky areas. Chaparral species intertongue with this woodland, usually on steep talus slopes.

The Wilson Mountain Trail (Red Rock Country Trail #9) provides an excellent tour of one of these park-like woodlands.

Riparian Communities: Probably the showiest vegetation type is the dense foliage on the banks of Oak Creek. The

Pinyon - Juniper Woodland

Evergreen Oak Woodland

Arizona Cypress Woodland

riparian or streamside vegetation is actually a series of overlapping communities which all need abundant and dependable supplies of water. In upper Oak Creek Canyon, the most apparent trees are New Mexico alder, box elder, bigtooth maple, sycamore, narrowleaf cottonwood, and velvet ash. Many members of the Ponderosa Pine-Fir Community invade this association, increasing plant species diversity significantly. Coffeeberry, red willow, arroyo willow, Arizona rose, grape, and Virginia creeper, mingle with patches of New Mexico raspberry, Himalaya berry, and red raspberry to form the dominant undergrowth. Giant horsetails, scouring rush, river sedge, beebalm and other mints, watercress, and yellow monkeyflower cover the muddy banks and grow in tight clumps on islands of soil in the stream itself. We shall call this group of riparian communities the Upper Riparian Community.

The riparian vegetation changes noticeably below the Bootlegger Campground. Greater insolation (sunlight) due to the increased width of the canyon and a broader floodplain is reflected in a shift of relative dominance toward Arizona sycamore, Fremont cottonwood, and Arizona walnut. New Mexico alder continues to occur but only in scattered dense stands. The understory is reduced considerably although grape, Virginia creeper, and most of the sedges and tall grasses remain. Nearing Sedona, mesquite, catclaw acacia, and seep willow begin to be added to the understory. This we shall call the Lower Riparian Community.

In other nearby canyons where streams are intermittent, the Riparian Communities vary sharply in composition and density. Generally the total availability of water will control which species will be present. Also, in these areas there is more encroachment by adjacent communities.

Desert-Grassland: Within the Red Rock Country this community is somewhat overshadowed by plants invading from the woodlands and chaparral. However, along the southern and western boundary of our area are some examples of Desert-Grassland. Where soil is deep and not rocky, perennial grasses such as black grama, sideoats grama, and hairy grama may be common. Other grasses include plains lovegrass, sand dropseed, and several kinds of three-awn grass. On the more shallow

Upper Riparian

Lower Riparian

Desert - Grassland

soils and gravelly hills and slopes are found ocotillo, prickly pear, cholla, false paloverde, wait-a-minute bush, catclaw acacia, narrowleaf yucca, and beargrass. Only the hardier grasses, such as fluff grass, may be present in the rockier soils. Much former Desert-Grassland has been encroached upon by less palatable snakeweed, tumbleweed, four-wing saltbush, and mesquite because the original grasses have been overgrazed by livestock.

Associated with these plant communities are, of course, complimentary populations of animals. Over 250 kinds of vertebrate ("having backbones") animals are known from this area. Additionally, thousands of species of insects and other invertebrates ("without backbones") can be found there. One especially important factor in attracting wildlife in this arid region is the dependable water supply of Oak Creek and West Fork.

Let us examine the common and/or typical vertebrate animals of each major plant community:

Ponderosa Pine-Fir Forest Fauna: There is only one amphibian that could be considered characteristic of this association in the Oak Creek Canyon area, namely, the Arizona treefrog. This tiny frog breeds primarily in shallow summer rain pools and may occasionally be found in trees to considerable heights.

No reptile is representative of this association, although the eastern fence lizard, short-horned lizard (often called horny toad but it is not an amphibian), and gopher snake may be common in specific areas. However, a number of birds are typical of this association. They include:

Flammulated Owl	Mountain Bluebird
Pygmy Owl	Townsend's Solitaire
Saw-whet Owl	Audubon's Warbler
Broad-tailed Hummingbird	Townsend's Warbler
Calliope Hummingbird	Hermit Warbler
Williamson's Sapsucker	Western Tanager
Hammond's Flycatcher	Evening Grosbeak
Olive-sided Flycatcher	Pine Siskin
Steller's Jay	Red Crossbill
Mountain Chickadee	Oregon Junco
Pygmy Nuthatch	Gray-headed Junco
Brown Creeper	

The mammals restricted, at least to some extent, to this association are:

Merriam's Shrew	Abert's Squirrel
Golden-mantled	Red Squirrel
Ground Squirrel	Wapiti or Elk
Gray-collared Chipmunk	Mule Deer

Chaparral Fauna: No snake or lizard is characteristic of or restricted to chaparral although densities may be high. For the most part, these reptiles are typical desert-grassland species, and here are reaching their upper altitudinal limits.

There are a few birds which show preference for this community; they are:

Orange-crowned Warbler	Lazuli Bunting
MacGillivray's Warbler	Rufous-sided Towhee

There are no mammals peculiar to the chaparral of North America, although rock squirrels and cliff chipmunks reach relatively large populations. Woodrats may also be common. Mule deer may migrate down into this association during the winter. The chaparral fauna, like that of the woodland, is largely ecotonal between montane forest and grassland or desert scrub.

Woodlands as Faunal Ecotones: Animal life of the woodland communities is not highly distinctive. Species of adjacent plant communities (i.e. montane forest edges, riparian situations, chaparral, etc.) penetrate into these woodlands to produce an ecotonal situation.

Rattlesnakes and a variety of lizards invade from nearby deserts, but are not particularly characteristic of the woodland itself.

Some of the birds to be found in the Woodland Communities are:

Band-tailed Pigeon	Pinyon Jay
Acorn Woodpecker	Plain Titmouse
Lewis' Woodpecker	Common Bushtit
Ash-throated Flycatcher	Bewick's Wren
Gray Flycatcher	Blue-gray Gnatcatcher
Scrub Jay	Black-throated Gray
Scott's Oriole	Warbler

No mammal is characteristic of woodland except perhaps the pinyon mouse which feeds extensively on pinyon nuts. Rock squirrels, cliff chipmunks, woodrats, and other mice are found here but any preference for woodland vegetation is superceded by the need for rocky hillsides and cliffs.

Riparian Fauna: Oak Creek and West Fork support a lush and varied riparian community. As described earlier, there exist a series of overlapping plant communities along the creeks. This diversity plus the close proximation of the other vegetative associations produces unusual mixtures of plants and animals. For instance, typical montane birds may be seen alongside typical desert riparian reptiles.

Certain animals are completely dependent upon the riparian areas. These would be, of course, most of the amphibians, including Woodhouse's toad, southwestern toad, tiger salamander, canyon treefrog, and leopard frog. The Sonoran mud turtle, western garter snake and the rare narrow-headed garter snake are restricted to the creek banks, also.

Birds that are largely limited to the riparian for nesting include:

Yellow-billed Cuckoo	Starling
Belted Kingfisher	Yellow Warbler
Gila Woodpecker	Yellowthroat
Ladder-backed Woodpecker	Yellow-breasted Chat
Western Kingbird	Painted Redstart
Cassin's Kingbird	Hooded Oriole
Weid's Crested Flycatcher	Bullock's Oriole
Black Phoebe	Summer Tanager
Bridled Titmouse	Lesser Goldfinch
Dipper	Mourning Dove
Robin	

The gray fox, striped skunk, raccoon, and ringtail are more common along the creek than elsewhere. Beaver and muskrat are restricted to the riparian zone. The Arizona gray squirrel appears to require the large deciduous trees for nest sites. Deer, wapiti, and coyote visit the creek for water at night, returning to the rim areas by daybreak. Many of the bats live in the cracks and caves along the canyon walls and feed on insects hovering above the stream.

Of the Red Rock Country's 250 species of vertebrates, over 60 per cent are dependent, for at least part of their life cycle, on the riparian zone.

Desert-Grassland Fauna: Although vegetatively over-shadowed by the Woodland and Chaparral communities, there are nonetheless many animals present considered to be typical of the Desert-Grassland.

Hammond's spadefoot toad is generally not seen nor heard until the summer rains begin. Then, at night, loud choruses are heard around temporary pools where breeding commences. By September, the pools have all dried and if lucky, the tadpoles have metamorphosed into toads just in time to burrow into the soil and remain dormant until the following summer.

Many reptiles inhabit this community. Some lizards commonly encountered include:

Texas Earless Lizard	Side-blotched Lizard
Clark's Spiny Lizard	Tree Lizard
Eastern Fence Lizard	

Snakes are less commonly encountered because of their nocturnal habits. However, many times on summer evenings a snake may be seen lying on paved highways that are warmer than the adjacent ground. Some to be expected include:

Striped Whipsnake	Western Diamondback
Western Patch-nosed Snake	Rattlesnake
Gopher Snake	Western Rattlesnake
Night Snake	Black-tailed Rattlesnake

Because of the lack of trees, birds of the Desert-Grassland either nest elsewhere and only forage in this community or are generally ground nesters. The former include the Turkey Vulture, Red-tailed Hawk, Golden Eagle, and Common Raven. These birds prefer a cliff or large tree for nesting but spend a great deal of time hunting or scavenging in the Desert-Grassland. Gambel's Quail, Roadrunner, Common Nighthawk, Horned Lark, and Black-throated Sparrow nest either directly on the ground or in a bush near ground level.

Mammals that might be encountered during the day include

blacktail jackrabbit, desert cottontail, and Harris' antelope squirrel. Common nocturnal mammals would be deer mice, coyotes, gray fox, and spotted skunks. Occasionally a desert shrew turns up in someone's house in Sedona.

Oak Creek and West Fork: The populations of fish occuring in Oak Creek and West Fork are, today, primarily artificial. The Arizona Game and Fish Department plant trout twice a week throughout the summer months. This amounts to some 150,000 rainbow trout, an average of 7500 per week.

The following native fishes should be present in the permanent drainages in small numbers:

Colorado Chub	Sonora Sucker
Speckled Dace	Gila Mountain-sucker
Spike Dace	

Historically, there were at least two other native fish. They were the Gila trout and the Colorado River squawfish.

The list of exotics or introduced fish is longer (see checklist) and possibly not complete, since there may be some aquarium type fishes present in portions of the Oak Creek drainages.

FURTHER READING

Aitchison, Stewart W. and Dennis S. Tomko. 1974. *Amphibians and reptiles of Flagstaff, Arizona.* Plateau, Vol. 47, No. 1:18-25.

Arnberger, Leslie P. 1962. *Flowers of the Southwest Mountains.* Southwestern Monuments Association, Popular Series #7. Globe, AZ. 112 pp.

Burt, William Henry. 1964. *A Field Guide to the Mammals.* Peterson Field Guide Series #5. Houghton Mifflin Co., Boston. 284 pp.

Dodge, Natt N. 1965. *Flowers of the Southwest Deserts.* Southwestern Monuments Association, Popular Series #4. Globe, AZ. 112 pp.

Little, Elbert L. 1968. *Southwestern Trees*. U.S. Dept. of Agriculture, Agriculture Handbook #9. Washington, D.C. 109 pp.

Lowe, Charles H. 1964. *Arizona's Natural Environment*. University of Arizon Press, Tucson. 136 pp.

McDougall, W.B. 1973. *Seed Plants of Northern Arizona*. Museum of Northern Arizona, Flagstaff. 594 pp.

Minkley. W.L. 1973. *Fishes of Arizona*. Arizona Game and Fish Dept. 293 pp.

Murie, Olans J. 1975. *A Field Guide to Animal Tracks*. Peterson Field Guide Series #9. Houghton Mifflin Co., Boston. 375 pp.

Patraw, Pauline M. 1953. *Flowers of the Southwestern Mesas*. Southwestern Monuments Association, Globe, AZ. 112 pp.

Phillips, Allan, Joe Marshall, and Gale Monson. 1964. *The Birds of Arizona*. University of Arizona Press, Tucson. 212 pp.

Stebbins, Robert C. 1966. *A Field Guide to Western Reptiles and Amphibians*. Peterson Field Guide Series #16. Houghton Mifflin Co., Boston. 279 pp.

RED ROCK COUNTRY TRAILS

This section is a guide to some of the roads and trails that traverse the Oak Creek Canyon-Red Rock Country area. Overnight camping is restricted to established campgrounds within Oak Creek Canyon. This rule was implemented because of the high concentration of use along Oak Creek and as an attempt to mitigate environmental degradation.

If you plan to camp outside the restricted area (Oak Creek Canyon proper), remember these suggestions:

1. Be sure you are on Forest Service land, not private property. A current Forest Service map is helpful.
2. Carry plenty of water. About one gallon per day per person in summer is recommended. There is no dependable water away from Oak Creek and West Fork.
3. Check with the Forest Service on current fire restrictions placed on the forest. If you build a campfire, do not leave a ring of blackened rocks and a pile of ashes and charred logs. Instead, scatter the rocks and bury the cold ashes. Return the area to its natural state. Better yet, use a camping stove.
4. Carry out all trash. Do not bury litter; animals only dig it up. Orange peels, egg shells, and many other food scraps do not decompose readily; please carry it *all* out.
5. Bury human waste at least six inches deep and far away from any water source. Burn your toilet paper. Be careful, though, so you do not start a forest fire.
6. Avoid camping in washes. Flash floods come unannounced.
7. Some trails are in poor condition, so allow plenty of time. Tell someone where you are going and when you expect to return.
8. Climbing on the soft sandstone and brittle limestone is DANGEROUS.
9. Do not attempt to cross Oak Creek while in flood. This condition arises often after a summer thunderstorm and during the spring snow-melt.

10. Drive only on established roads, leave gates as you find them, open or closed, and park so as not to block the road.

Of great help when exploring the backcountry are good, detailed maps. By far the best are the United States Geological Survey Topographic Maps available sometimes locally or from the Branch of Distribution, United States Geological Survey, Box 25286, Denver, Colorado 80225. The U.S. Forest Service also has maps available that show some trails and Forest Service roads. These maps also have the road numbers that most of the Forest Service roads are marked with instead of place name signs. Write to or stop by either of these offices:

Coconino National Forest   Sedona Ranger Station
Forest Supervisor's Office   or P. O. Box 300
2323 Greenlaw Lane   651 Hwy. 179
Flagstaff, AZ 86001   Sedona, AZ 86336

The five road logs cover two paved highways and three dirt-gravel roads. The latter can usually be negotiated by ordinary passenger cars provided one drives slowly. An exceptionally hard rain or snowstorm would, of course, make these routes difficult if not impossible. The Schnebly Hill Road is usually snowpacked above the rim from December through March.

The foot or pack trail descriptions have the following format:

1. Trail number - this is my own numbering system.
2. Name of trail, alternate names and/or U.S. Forest Service numbers given in parentheses.
3. Trailhead location - this is given as township, range, and section for quick location on the topo or Forest Service map. Additional location descriptions are given in the first paragraph of each trail's discussion section.
4. Trailhead elevation, total vertical ascent, highest point, and length (one way) are self-explanatory.
5. Maps - appropriate topo and Forest Service maps are listed. Trails are *not* always shown but nevertheless maps are a handy item.

All road distances from Sedona are measured from the junction of highways 89A and 179.

ROAD LOGS

ROAD LOG #1

Highway 89A: Oak Creek View Point to Sedona

Mile

0.0   Oak Creek View Point (el. 6407 ft.). Principal vegetation consists of ponderosa pine, Gambel's oak, mountain mahogany, manzanita, Rocky Mountain juniper, and shrub live oak. High flat-topped mesa to the south (down canyon) on skyline is Wilson Mountain (el. 7076 ft.). Note that the western rim is over 500 ft. higher than the east rim because of faulting. Rocks exposed in the west wall are (top to bottom) partly concealed buff Kaibab Limestone, prominent cliff of white Toroweap Sandstone, larger cliff of Coconino Sandstone grading in color from yellow down to red. To the east (left) is Pumphouse Canyon. Presumably water was pumped up the wash for use by a lumber mill's railroad. Canyon walls are formed of black lava (basalt) on top, forest-covered slope partly conceals Kaibab Limestone and cliff of Toroweap Sandstone. Highway zigzags down 1500 feet in the next 2.2 miles, passing through a series of dark lava flows separated by beds of red clay that may indicate former soil zones. Drive carefully.

0.8   Lava flow to right of road shows columnar structure (six-sided columns) formed during cooling. Individual columns average about 2 ft. thick and 30 ft. high.

0.9   Contact between black lava and buff Kaibab Limestone on right side of road. Limestone surface shows erosion and channeling developed before volcanic activity covered it. At road turn, rocks are shattered and fractured along line at fault.

1.3   Canyon wall to left of road is formed of thick beds of Kaibab Limestone. Contains layers of white chert or

Road in Lower Oak Creek Canyon — early 1900's

flint-like rock as well as marine fossils.

1.7   At right, yellowish-white Toroweap sandstone shows conspicuously sloping layers of sand deposited presumably by water currents.

1.9   Sterling Spring State Fish Hatchery. Principal spring supplying water to Oak Creek is 1/4 mile up canyon at right. Water issues from Coconino Sandstone where rock has been fractured in a fault zone.

2.2   Bridge over Pumphouse Wash. From bridge to Pine Flat Campground, the forest on the left is composed of ponderosa pine, Douglas fir, and Gambel's oak. In spring the wildflower blue lupine is common. On right the forest is composed of Douglas fir, white fir, box elder, New Mexico alder, narrowleaf cottonwood, Arizona walnut, Gambel's oak, and scarlet sumac.

3.1   Pine Flat Campground. Note black bark on young ponderosa pines; as they approach an age of 200 years the bark will turn yellow-brown. Fine spring water is available at roadside rock structure.

3.7   Harding Springs on right bank of creek. Box elder is abundant; so is arroyo willow, watercress, monkeyflower, dogwood, scouring rush, grape, and various sedges.

4.0   First farm plots and orchards to be seen in canyon appear on right. Excellent view of Toroweap-Coconino cliffs with red Supai Sandstone at base.

4.2   Harding Springs Trail (Red Rock Country Trail #1) ascends canyon wall on left. Entrance to Cave Spring Campground on right (Red Rock Country Trail #2).

4.4   Toroweap on left shows cross-bedding.

5.1   This area is the setting for Zane Grey's novel "Call of the Canyon," and he lived here while writing the book.

5.6   Mayhew's Lodge, on canyon floor at right, is located at the mouth of West Fork of Oak Creek. West Fork has been set aside by the Forest Service as a Natural Area (Red Rock Country Trail #3). Sycamore trees now become prominent along the creek. Also found are Douglas fir, white fir, arroyo willow, New Mexico alder, box elder, narrowleaf cottonwood, scarlet sumac, raspberry, and many non-native plants such as tree-of-heaven and apple trees.

5.7   West wall cliff contains exceptional exposure of Coconino Sandstone developed through accumulation of wind-blown (eolian) sand. This sand was deposited by wind blowing from the north.

6.9   Bootlegger (formerly Slide Rock) Campground. Across creek, A. B. Young or East Pocket Trail (Red Rock Country Trail #4) switchbacks up west wall to rim.

7.3   Five dikes (vertical sheets) of black basalt project through the buff Coconino Sandstone to the left of the road above and below Junipine Store. The dikes are about 2 1/2 feet thick and can be traced upward to a lava flow on canyon rim. They fill the conduits through which volcanic materials reached the surface.

7.5   Banjo Bill Campground contains a scrubby growth of Arizona walnut, New Mexico locust, shrub live oak, alligator-bark juniper, silk-tassel, mountain mahogany, box elder, and sycamore. Near here, east wall of canyon is formed of a thick series of dark lava flows.

8.0   Half Way Picnic Ground.

8.7   Highway crosses bridge. Slide Rock, a favorite swimming place, is located slightly upstream. Note signs about water pollution when number of users exceeds 250 people! Good views of Supai Sandstone on west wall. Eastern slopes are typical chaparral-type plant communities which consist of manzanita, shrub live oak, silk-tassel, barberry and other shrubs.

9.1   Natural arch on right in Supai. Blackberry along road.

9.6   Manzanita Campground. Scarlet sumac on right side of road. Ponderosa pine, evergreen oaks, and Arizona walnut trees in camp.

10.1   Encinoso Picnic Area. Very scenic trail (Red Rock Country Trail #6) to Wilson Mountain begins just north of picnic area.

11.7   Munds Canyon enters on left.

11.8   Indian Gardens, former site of a Yavapai Indian community. First American settler in Oak Creek Canyon built cabin here in 1876. Note wild grape and poison ivy. During summer many roadside wildflowers from here south, notably globe mallow, red and pink penstemons, wild rhubarb, prickly poppy, peppergrass, loco weed, purple nightshade, sacred datura, and indigobush. Supposedly an ancient Indian trail climbed west out of Oak Creek Canyon over to Sterling Canyon and the upper Dry Creek area.

12.7   First good views of spectacular rock formations consisting of buttes of the "A" member of the Supai Sandstone. Among these is Mitten Ridge.

12.9   High up to left, Schnebly Hill Road can be seen winding down from the east rim. Narrow inner canyon is formed by the "C" member of the Supai Formation. First large stands of Arizona cypress trees visible.

13.0   Casner Canyon Trail (Red Rock Trail #7) is to the east of the creek.

13.4   To left, Allen's Bend Trail (Red Rock Country Trail #8) is located one-tenth mile down Grasshopper Point Road.

14.0   Midgley Bridge, named for Major Midgley who advocated its construction. Wilson Mountain Trail (Red Rock Country Trail #9) begins on east side of bridge. Excellent trail to view the Arizona cypress forest. Many sugar sumac bushes in area.

14.2   Steamboat Rock on right.

14.8   Canotia or false paloverde to right.

15.9   Junction of highway 89A and 179. Sedona (el. 4200 ft.),
       named for Sedona Schnebly, one of the early settlers,
       is a thriving resort area, art center, and hub of fruit-
       growing and ranching activities. The town is almost
       encircled by buttes and hills of the red Supai Sandstone,
       some known locally as "Steamboat" (north) and "The
       Thumb" (northeast). To the north and east is main
       plateau with cliffs of white Coconino and Toroweap
       Sandstones rising above the red rocks. Black lavas from
       canyon rim in distance. To the south, Courthouse Rock,
       (incorrectly shown on the topographic and Forest Service
       maps as Cathedral) is a conspicuous landmark. Oak
       Creek (below at left) has incised its course below general
       ground level and is marked by a narrow belt of
       sycamores and other riparian (stream-side) plants.

ROAD LOG #2

Highway 179: Sedona to Woods Canyon Turnoff

Mile

0.0   Start at junction of highways 89A and 179 in Sedona.
0.3   Bridge over Oak Creek; Schnebly Hill Road to left.
1.5   Turn off to left for Red Rock Country Trail #10.
1.6   Sedona District Ranger Station on right; road travels
       through a pinyon pine and one-seed juniper woodland
       with a thick chaparral understory. As we go south, the
       chaparral is slowly replaced with more desert-grassland
       species. Also the pinyon pine becomes more scarce and
       the juniper is more widely spaced due to lower soil
       moisture.
3.3   Most maps show the rock tower on right as Cathedral
       Rock but it was first named Courthouse Butte in 1886.
4.5   The large blockish butte on the left is cut by a fault. The
       southern portion is Lee Mountain; the northern part is

Munds Mountain.

4.8   Oldtimers say that Cathedral (or Church) Rock is on left although modern maps are labeled Courthouse Butte.

5.1   Scenic pull-out on right.

5.3   Bell Rock on left.

6.4   Big Park. Where developers and subdivisions have not disturbed the ground, it is fairly typical desert-grassland although the abundance of catclaw acacia, mesquite, snakeweed, and narrowleaf yucca is probably due to previous overgrazing by livestock. This overgrazing and heavy rains near the turn of the century caused most of the deep arroyos (washes) to be formed.

6.5   Turn-off to left for Red Rock Country Trail #11.

7.2   Pond on right attracts migrating ducks and geese.

8.6   Turnoff through gate to Woods Canyon and Hot Loop Trails (Red Rock Country Trails #12 and #13) on left.

ROAD LOG #3

Schnebly Hill Road: Sedona to the Mogollon Rim

Mile

0.0   Start at junction of highway 179 and Schnebly Hill Road (see Road Log #2).

0.5   Cattleguard across road and end of pavement. Schnebly Hill Road was built by the Schneblys, founders of the Sedona post office, and other Sedona residents about 1902. It was a partial improvement and realignment of the old Munds horse trail. When first completed, this road was the most direct route from Sedona to Flagstaff. Sedona-grown fruits and vegetables were taken to the Flagstaff market and lumber and other manufactured goods brought back.

0.9   Arizona Cypress Woodland becomes dominant. Many movies have been made in this area, such as "Broken Arrow" and "The Last Wagon."

1.2   Beautiful vista of the Sedona area. Good exposure of the Supai Formation.

3.0   Fremont cottonwood trees can be seen on the left growing near the intermittent streambed. They require more moisture than cypress or juniper and usually indicate that water is near the surface.

3.4   Some of the Arizona cypress here is heavily infested with mistletoe. Mistletoe is a parasitic plant living off the mutrients produced by the host plant, in this case, the cypress. The berries produced by mistletoe are eaten by birds who in turn land and defecate the seeds on other trees, thus spreading the parasite.

4.5   Fort Apache Limestone member of the Supai Formation forms the flat shelf-like structure to the left of the road. This particular rock formation is locally called "The Merry-go-round."

5.0   Note natural "window" at left in Supai.

5.4   Cliffrose is common along right side of road. This is an important browse plant for deer.

5.5   From here is a good view of the Casner Canyon Trail (Red Rock Country Trail #7) climbing steeply up the canyon wall to the north. Also note Wilson Mountain to the west with its "bench." This relatively level area is the result of a block of Wilson Mountain being down-faulted. Also, it is on that bench where the Wilson Mountain Trail and the North Wilson Trail (Red Rock Country Trails #9 and #6) intersect.

5.7   Chaparral vegetation is predominant in this area.

5.9   This drainage must be slightly cooler and wetter than the adjacent slopes to support the bigtooth maple, box elder, Douglas fir, New Mexico locust, and Gambel's oak. The buff cross-bedded Coconino Sandstone overlain by dark black basalt can be seen, too.

6.4   One-seed juniper makes its appearance.

8.1   You are now on top of the Mogollon Rim and are entering the ponderosa pine forest.

11.5   Interstate Highway 17; turn left to Flagstaff, right to Camp Verde and Phoenix.

ROAD LOG #4

Dry Creek - Boynton Pass Roads

Mile

0.0   Start at junction of highway 89A and 179 in Sedona. Drive west (toward Cottonwood) on 89A.

3.1   Turn right (north) on Dry Creek Road, Forest Service Road #152.

4.7   End of pavement. The principal vegetation is pinyon pine, one-seed juniper, manzanita, shrub live oak, snake-weed, tumbleweed, graythorn, prickly pear, banana yucca, and grasses. House Finches and Scrub Jays are common.

5.2   Sterling Canyon Road, Forest Service Road #152C, turns off to right. This road leads to Red Rock Country Trails 16 through 19. Vegetation is about same as last stop, but now an occasional barberry bush is noticed.

5.5   View to the west of magnificent cliffs of Supai, Coconino and Toroweap. The contact between the Coconino and Toroweap is defined by a thin horizontal line of vegetation.

5.8   Many more Arizona cypress trees intermingling.

6.0   Road crosses Dry Creek. If there is flowing water deeper than one foot, do not attempt to ford it. It is in this drainage system that evidence of the earliest known human occupants of the Red Rock Country was found. This evidence consists mainly of primitive stone tools which may be 4000 years old.

6.1   Long Canyon Road to right provides access to Red Rock Country Trail #20. Left to Boynton Pass.

6.6   Arizona cypress thins out and is replaced by pinyon pine and one-seed juniper. Cypress is restricted to drainages on cooler slopes.

6.8   Note shrub that looks similar to the shrub live oak except leaves are shiny and yellow-green and broader. This is Palmer oak.

8.2   Turn off on right to Fay Canyon Arch, Red Rock Country Trail #21. The small yucca is narrowleaf yucca. At the edge of the clearing note the large Emory oak, squaw-bush, banana yucca, barberry, and a clump of soapberry trees.

8.6   Boynton Pass. Jerome, an old copper-mining town, is perched on the distant mountain. The chaparral understory thins and is replaced by more of the desert-grassland plants such as snakeweed, catclaw, and narrowleaf yucca.

9.5   Marshall Tank on left. The tall trees are Fremont cottonwoods.

9.6   Keep left.

9.7   Keep right.

11.7   Junction with Forest Service Road #525. Turn left. Right takes you to Red Rock Country Trail #22. Plants include one-seed juniper, snakeweed, prickly pear, catclaw acacia, and mesquite. Pictographs on the cliffs to the north indicate that the Yavapai-Apache once lived in the area.

12.9   Canotia or false paloverde becomes apparent.

14.7   Turnoff to right goes to Mooney Trail (Red Rock Country Trail #23), Casner Mountain Trail (Red Rock Country Trail #24), and eventually Sycamore Pass, where one can enter the Sycamore Canyon Wilderness Area. The junipers here are small and well spaced, which indicates low soil moisture. Also note four-wing saltbush and tumbleweed growing in the disturbed soil along the road.

17.4   Junction with Highway 89A. Turn right to Cottonwood; left to Sedona.

ROAD LOG #5

Red Rock Loop Road

Mile

0.0   Start at junction of highways 89A and 179 in Sedona. Drive west (toward Cottonwood) on 89A.

4.2   Turn left (south) on Red Rock Loop Road, Forest Service Road #216. This drive goes through a primarily pinyon pine and one-seed juniper woodland with a chaparral understory which is replaced by a desert-grassland understory on the more arid slopes. Typical species include mesquite, catclaw, barberry, shrub live oak, snakeweed, squawbush, prickly pear, narrowleaf yucca, banana yucca, and false paloverde.

6.2   The Red Rock Loop Road is the right branch. As the road continues around Schuerman Mountain, one passes many lovely homes overlooking Oak Creek. Take left fork, Forest Service Road #216A, for a sidetrip of about a mile to Red Rock Crossing and a picnic area. Large sycamores and cottonwoods shade Oak Creek and Cathedral or Courthouse Rock looms in the background. Oldtimers say that the modern maps are wrong and that three-part butte is really called Courthouse Rock not Cathedral according to General Land Office surveys done in 1886.

7.5   Red Rock Loop Road crosses wash. Note the large Goodding willow on left and the abundant seep willows.

11.6   As you near the junction with Highway 89A, look up to the right and there is a natural "window" in the Supai Formation. At 89A, right will take you back to Sedona; left to Cottonwood.

FOOT TRAILS

Red Rock Country Trail #1

Name: Harding Springs Trail (Hart; USFS #51)
Trailhead location: T.19N., R.6E., Sec. 27
Trailhead elevation: 5448 feet
Total vertical ascent: about 900 feet
Highest point: about 6300 feet
Length (one way): about .75 miles
Maps: 7.5' Mountainaire; 7.5' Munds Park; Coconino National
*Forest (north half); trail is shown **only** on Forest Service*
map.

This trail is about 11.7 miles north of the junction of highway 89A and 179 in Sedona. The trailhead is opposite the Cave Spring Campground entrance on 89A and is marked by a small wooden sign. As with many of the Oak Creek Canyon trails, the Harding Springs Trail was built to provide access to the rim for early settlers who wanted a shorter route to Flagstaff and points beyond. Probably originally built by settler J. R. Robinson in the early 1880's, it was used and maintained by succeeding owners Dave Hart in 1883, and Col. O. P. Harding after 1893.

The springs mentioned in the name of the trail probably refer to the water source about .4 of a mile north of the trailhead on the west bank of Oak Creek (see Road Log #1).

The trail ascends through a moist ponderosa pine forest with some Douglas fir, bigtooth maples, and New Mexico locust. Steller's Jays and Mountain Chickadees are common. A sharp-eyed observer might see a Brown Creeper gleaning the bark of a conifer. Also, cliff chipmunks populate the area.

Upon nearing the rim, more arid conditions are found and alligator-bark juniper, large specimens of agave, and Gambel's oak become more prevalent. Once on the rim, a good view both up and down canyon is obtained. One can follow the rim south about one-half mile to encounter a primitive Forest Service road.

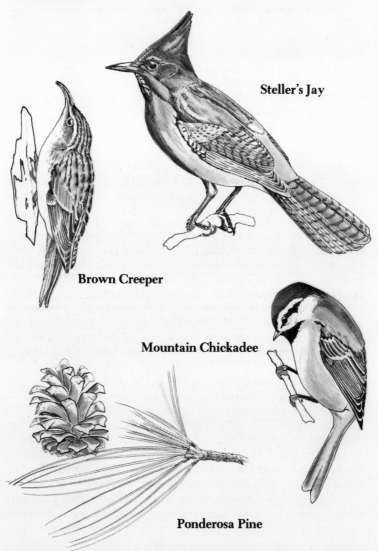

Steller's Jay

Brown Creeper

Mountain Chickadee

Ponderosa Pine

Red Rock Country Trail #2

Name: Cave Springs Nature Trail
Trailhead location: T.19N., R.6E., Sec. 27
Trailhead elevation: 5400 feet
Total vertical ascent: negligible
Length (one way): .5 miles
Maps: 7.5' Mountainaire; 7.5' Munds Park; Coconino National
*   Forest (north half); trail not shown on the maps.*

This trail is located at the north end of the Cave Spring Campground which is about 11.7 miles north of Sedona on Highway 89A. This is a very easy walk, but allow 15 to 30 minutes to relax and enjoy the scenery. The Forest Service has placed small signs identifying some of the common trees and shrubs. A spring used to flow out of the small cave in the Coconino formation, but today has been capped for use by the campground. Note the Black Phoebe nests clinging to the cave's walls. During spring and early summer, this area is a favorite haunt for birdwatchers. Over 40 species have been sighted here including the Band-tailed Pigeon, Flammulated Owl, White-throated Swift, Belted Kingfisher, Yellow-bellied Sapsucker, Dipper, Pygmy Nuthatch, American Redstart, Painted Redstart, Black-headed Grosbeak, and Indigo Bunting.

Arizona Gray Squirrel

Three species of tree squirrels inhabit the campground area. They are the Abert's squirrel, Arizona gray squirrel, and red squirrel. Normally these three are not found together because of their fairly specific diets; the Abert's squirrel prefering

Abert's Squirrel

Red Squirrel

ponderosa pine, the Arizona gray squirrel liking walnuts, and the red squirrel requiring spruce and firs. However, these four kinds of trees all occur in the campground area.

Red Rock Country Trail #3

Name: West Fork Trail (USFS #108)
Trailhead location: T.19N., R.6E., Sec. 34
Trailhead elevation: 5280 feet
Total vertical ascent: 1220 feet
Highest point: 6500 feet
Length (one way): about 12 miles from Forest Service Road
*   #231 to Oak Creek*
Maps: 7.5' Dutton Hill; 7.5' Munds Park; 7.5' Wilson Mountain;
*   Coconino National Forest (north half); no trail shown*
*   on maps*

The charm of the stream, the sublimity of the towering Coconino and Toroweap cliffs, and the luxuriant riparian vegetation all combine to make this one of the most memorable hikes in Oak Creek Canyon. The West Fork of Oak Creek is located 10.3 miles north of Sedona at Mayhew's Lodge. Parking is limited to several wide shoulders along the highway. Be sure to pull off completely, and do not block any of the drive-ways.

Because of the stream's fragile nature and heavy use on weekends, the lower six stream miles are *closed* to overnight camping and campfires. If you refer to the Dutton Hill topo map, the upper end of the no camping area is about due north of East Buzzard Point.

(Courtesy of Northern Arizona Pioneer's Historical Society, Northern Arizona University Library, Special Collections)

Mayhew's Lodge — 1908

Most hikers do a day-long trip by beginning at Mayhew's Lodge [the lodge is currently closed to the public; please note USFS signs] and walking and wading up West Fork one to several miles and then returning. There is a definite trail only for the first mile or so; after that the canyon walls fairly well limit where one can walk. An overnight trip can be done provided you are prepared to hike, wade, and possibly swim past the six-mile boundary for your night's camp. Some backpackers prefer to begin at the upper end of West Fork, where Forest Service road #231 crosses it. The first six miles or so are usually dry. The first permanent water is approximately located below East Buzzard Point and should be your camp. Be sure to carry a backpacking stove since fire wood is scarce and does provide nesting and foraging places for some of the smaller creatures. Bury human waste as far away from the stream as possible.

Carry out all garbage. *Do not attempt this trip if there is flowing water in the upper six miles or if rain is a possibility.* There is no place to run to if a wall of water comes screaming down the canyon.

Southwestern Toad

Leopard Frog

Canyon Treefrog

Woodhouse's Toad

Narrow-headed Garter Snake

Western Garter Snake

West Fork supports a lush growth of riparian plants. Golden columbine, larkspur, wild onion, buttercup, yellow monkey-flower, penstemon, and cone flower are only a few of the many beautiful wildflowers to be seen. Cottonwood, box elder, New Mexico alder, hoptree, walnut, ponderosa pine, Douglas fir, Engelmann spruce, and other trees compose the canopy. Even an occasional blue spruce grows in the upper reaches of the canyon.

Some trout occur in West Fork but few of catchable size. Several common amphibians include the tiger salamander, Woodhouse's toad, canyon treefrog, and the leopard frog. One amphibian living in the Red Rock Country is only known from West Fork. This is the southwestern toad whose range in the Southwest has become more and more broken because of increased aridity of the region during the last 12,000 years.

Two kinds of snakes are likely to be encountered, the narrow-headed garter snake and the western garter snake; both are harmless. Like the southwestern toad, the narrow-headed garter snake's range is today very localized in the Southwest.

The descending notes of the Canyon Wren are frequently heard but this diminutive denizen of the canyon walls is seldom seen. Along the stream the Belted Kingfisher and the Dipper feed on the abundant small minnows and aquatic invertebrates. Many typically riparian and forest birds breed in the canyon.

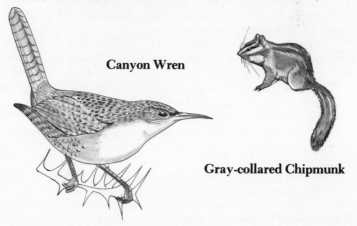

Canyon Wren

Gray-collared Chipmunk

Although lion and bear have been reported from West Fork, cliff and gray-collared chipmunks are far more likely to be encountered. Also Abert's squirrel with its "tufted ears" may be observed and its ratchet-like call occasionally permeates the usually quiet, still air. Ringtail "cats," actually a close relative of the raccoon, may try to steal your food at night, so sleep close to your pack.

Red Rock Country Trail #4

Name: East Pocket Trail (A. B. Young; USFS #100)
Trailhead location: T.18N., R.6E., Sec. 5
Trailhead elevation: 5160 feet
Total vertical ascent: 1537 feet to rim; 2063 feet to East Pocket
     Knob Lookout Tower
Highest point: 7196 feet at Lookout Tower
Length (one way): about 1.4 miles to rim; 2.6 miles to Lookout
     Tower
Maps: 7.5' Wilson Mountain; 7.5' Munds Park; Coconino
     National Forest (north half)

The trailhead is west of Bootlegger (formerly Slide Rock) Campground about 9 miles north of Sedona. Do not attempt to cross Oak Creek while in flood.

From several points along Highway 89A, this trail can be seen switchbacking up a chaparral covered slope to the west rim. It was originally built as a cattle trail and later improved as a Civilian Conservation Corps project in the 1930's. It offers fine views both up and down Oak Creek Canyon and also allows access to the south rim of West Fork. Following the trail southwestward from the west rim, one eventually reaches the East Pocket Knob Fire Lookout, which is maintained during the summer months.

Manzanita, shrub live oak, silk-tassel bush and other typically chaparral species compose the vegetation. An almost cat-like call is commonly heard along the trail; it belongs to the Rufous-sided Towhee, a permanent resident of the chaparral zone.

Rufous-sided Towhee

Shrub Live Oak

Red Rock Country Trail #5

Name: Purtymun Trail
Trailhead location: T.18N., R.6E., Sec. 8
Trailhead elevation: 5120 feet
Total vertical ascent: 1280 feet
Highest point: 6400 feet
Length (one way): about 1 mile
Maps: 7.5' Munds Park; 7.5' Wilson Mountain; Coconino
National Forest (south half); trail not shown on the maps.

About 8.6 miles north of Sedona, just about opposite the Junipine store, the Purtymun Trail ascends the east wall (only 300 to 400 feet of trail near the rim is recognizable; the remainer is overgrown). This trail was built about 1890 by a pioneer family by the name of Purtymun. As with many of these creek to rim trails, a wagon would be left at the top and the stock animals brought down into the canyon. then when it was time to go to Flagstaff again, up the trail with your animals, hitch them to the wagon and follow the wagon road into town. This

Old Trail into Oak Creek Canyon — 1894

"road" to Flagstaff approximately followed the present-day alignment of Interstate Highway 17.

Other trails in Oak Creek Canyon that were built for a similar purpose include the Thomas Trail, located approximately across from the mouth of West Fork; Thompson's Ladder Trail at the mouth of Munds Canyon; and Falls (Harrington) Trail on the east wall opposite Oak Creek Falls. These and still others have since fallen to disuse and/or are wholely or partially located on private land, so are no longer of recreational interest, and are mentioned only for their historical value.

Red Rock Country Trail #6

Name: North Wilson Trail (Encinoso, USFS #123)
Trailhead location: T.18N., R.6E., Sec. 21
Trailhead elevation: 4720 feet
Total vertical ascent: 1520 feet, to junction with Wilson Mountain Trail
Highest point: 6240 feet
Length (one way): about 1.75 miles
Maps: 7.5' Munds Park; Coconino National Forest (south half); trail not shown on either map

Park in the Encinoso Picnic Area, 5.8 miles north of Sedona on Highway 89A. The trailhead is a few hundred feet north of the picnic area and next to the highway.

This is a delightful trail in the summer because of its abundant cool shade, perhaps one of the nicest walks in Oak Creek Canyon. it begins in a woodland of evergreen oak (Encinoso is Spanish for "place of the evergreen oak"), alligator-bark juniper, agave, yucca, indigobush, manzanita, squawbush, and hollyleaf buckthorn. As the trail gains elevation and becomes more protected by the canyon walls, the vegetation changes to a ponderosa pine forest. Note that on your right the south facing wall is covered by chaparral vegetation, suggesting a more arid environment. Also listen for the shrill whistle of the rock squirrel. At about one-half mile from the picnic area

Hollyleaf Buckthorn

Rock Squirrel

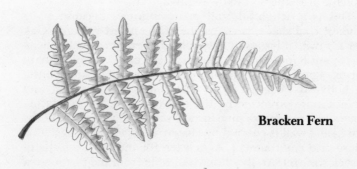

Bracken Fern

Alligator-bark Juniper

One-seed Juniper

Utah Juniper

the trail turns into a narrow, steep-walled canyon containing bigtooth maple, ponderosa pine, Douglas fir, white fir, New Mexico locust, hoptree, and bracken fern. A series of steep switchbacks takes one to the top of the First Bench of Wilson Mountain. This bench was formed by a huge block of Wilson Mountain being down-faulted relative to the western portion of the mountain. It is this same fault that has caused the formation and isolation of seven smaller hills along the west bank of Oak Creek. Look to the isolated hill to the north to see another example.

A fall hike will usually reveal many migrating species of birds. For instance, you might see Robins, Golden-crowned Kinglets, Western Bluebirds, and Bridled Titmice. Permanent residents include Red-shafted Flickers, Yellow-bellied Sapsuckers, Rufous-sided Towhees, and Steller's Jays.

Nearing the top of First Bench more silk-tassel bush, alligator-bark juniper, and mountain mahogany are encountered. Once on top the vegetation is more open, consisting mainly of annuals and grasses, small stands of stunted Gambel's oak, and an occasional one-seed, alligator-bark or Utah juniper.

The tops of First Bench and Wilson Mountain are covered with basaltic lava flows dating from late Pliocene times or about 5 million years ago.

Red Rock Country Trail #7

Name: Casner Canyon Trail (USFS #11)
Trailhead location: T.18N., R.6E., Sec. 33
Trailhead elevation: 4440 feet
Total vertical ascent: 1560 feet
Highest point: 6000 feet
Length (one way): about 2 miles
Maps: 7.5' Munds Park; Coconino National Forest (south half)

Drive 2.9 miles north of Sedona and park on the highway shoulder. To find the trailhead, first walk down the short dirt road shown on the topo map. a faint trail turns toward Oak

Squawbush

Buckbrush

Creek just before the road reaches a small building. The idea is to reach the creek, cross it (this may involve wading in 2 or 3 foot deep, swift-moving water) and then locate the drainage the trail ascends as shown on the topo map. Once at the mouth of this tributary the trail is more recognizable. A few hundred feet from Oak Creek, the Casner Canyon Trail crosses the unnamed tributary to the north side and remains there all the way to the rim.

At the base of this trail are some very large Arizona cypress trees. As the trail ascends, its southern exposure causes a chaparral type of vegetation to be dominant. Sugar sumac, shrub live oak, barberry, squawbush, manzanita, and false paloverde are common. Higher on the trail, the chaparral continues but the species composition changes slightly with more grasses, hollyleaf buckthorn, prickly pear, some juniper, pinyon pine, buckbrush, and less manzanita.

Rufous-sided Towhees and Gambel's Quail can be expected. Watch for hawks soaring over the canyon. A rarely seen lizard, the Sonoran skink, was observed on this trail near the top one warm October afternoon.

Nice vistas are obtained of the Sedona-Verde Valley area. Also near the rim are very good examples of columnar jointing in the basaltic lava flow.

Schnebly Hill Road can be reached by walking south one-half mile.

There were a number of Casners living in the Red Rock Country in the late 1800's. It is hard to say which one is commemorated by this trail, but Mose Casner was one of the more colorful figures of the time. He supposedly had gold in dutch ovens hidden here and there throughout the canyon.

Red Rock Country Trail #8

Name: Allen's Bend Trail (Grasshopper Point, USFS #111)
Trailhead location: T.17N., R.6E., Sec. 4
Trailhead elevation: 4530 feet
Total vertical ascent: 170 feet
Highest point: 4530 feet
Length (one way): .7 mile
Maps: 7.5' Munds Park; Coconino National Forest (south half)

This trail named after Charles Allen, a former owner of the Junipine Lodge, is an old, closed road taking off one-tenth mile down the Grasshopper Point Road, about 2.5 miles north of Sedona. It is an easy, short walk down to the creek. Plants found along the way are pinyon pine, one-seed juniper, sugar sumac, prickly pear, shrub live oak, yucca, buckbrush, barberry, and agave. At creek side there are a couple of ponderosa pines, quite a few sycamores, New Mexico alder, hoptree, and evergreen oaks. It is not unusual to see a Great Blue Heron wading and feeding along the shore.

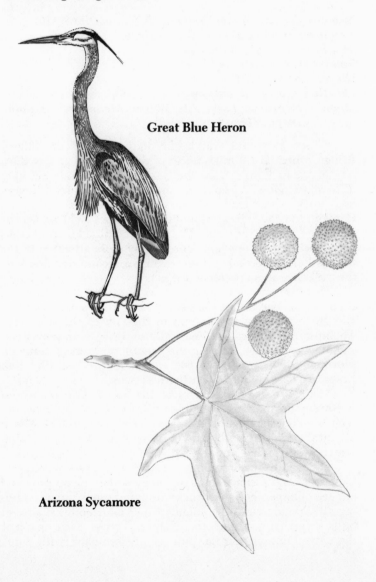

Great Blue Heron

Arizona Sycamore

Red Rock Country Trail #9

Name: Wilson Mountain Trail (South Wilson, USFS #10)
Trailhead location: T.17N., R.6E., Sec. 4
Trailhead elevation: 4520 feet
Total vertical ascent: 2440 feet
Highest point: 6960 feet
Length (one way): about 3 miles
Maps: 7.5' Munds Park; 7.5' Wilson Mountain; Coconino
*   National Forest (south half)*

Wilson Mountain Trail begins on the east side of Midgley Bridge, which is 1.9 miles north of Sedona on Highway 89A. About one-half mile from the beginning, the trail becomes difficult to follow. A jeep road comes in on the left from Steamboat Rock, a foot trail continues up the dry creek of Wilson Canyon, but the Wilson Mountain Trail goes right across the creek bed and up the slope. The way is confused by numerous paths for the next one-half mile, so pay close attention to the Munds Park topo map. After crossing a second dry drainage the trail once again becomes distinct.

This trail provides excellent views of the Red Rock Country. From on top, one can see the Verde Valley to the south, Schnebly Hill Road winding its way up to the rim to the southeast, Thompson's Ladder Trail (partially on private property) zig-zagging up to the wall at the mouth of Mund's Canyon, Mormon Mountain far to the east, and the beautiful San Francisco Peaks along the northern horizon.

There are good exposures of the Supai, Coconino, and Toroweap Formations. The top of Wilson Mountain is covered with late Pliocene basaltic lava flows. The First Bench of Wilson Mountain was originally part of the summit of Wilson Mountain; however, it has since been down-faulted as a huge block.

The trail begins in mainly an Arizona cypress Woodland. Other plants present are agave, yucca, some pinyon pine and one-seed juniper, hollyleaf buckthorn, and sugar sumac. Gaining altitude increases the abundance of manzanita, silk-tassel bush, shrub live oak, and other chaparral types. Once on top of the mountain, ponderosa pine is predominant with some

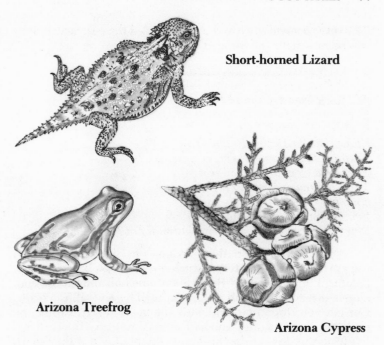

Short-horned Lizard

Arizona Treefrog

Arizona Cypress

Gambel's oak.

The raucous call of the Scrub Jay is frequently heard. Also look for the large common Raven and a soaring Red-tail Hawk or possibly a Golden Eagle. Mule deer may be encountered topside and coyote sign is prevalent. On one August day baby horned lizards seemed to be everywhere. In the ponderosa pine in early summer, the Arizona treefrog emerges from underground to breed in the temporary rain pools. During this breeding period, they may spend the day high in pine trees resting and eating bark beetles and other insects.

Wilson Canyon and Mountain are named in honor of Arkansas bear hunter Richard Wilson. One day in June, 1885, Wilson decided to go after a huge grizzly bear whose tracks he had seen between Sedona and Indian Gardens. Wilson's large caliber rifle was being repaired so he only had a small one to use. Nine days later, Wilson's mauled, decomposing body was found by two horsemen not far up what is now called Wilson

Canyon. Apparently, he had only wounded the bear and Wilson was no match for the enraged animal.

Red Rock Country Trail #10

Name: Devil's Dining Room Trail
Trailhead location: T.17N., R.6E., Sec. 20
Trailhead elevation: 4280 feet
Total vertical ascent: 80 feet
Highest point: 4360 feet
Length (one way): .5 mile
Maps: 7.5' Sedona; Coconino National Forest (south half)

About 1.5 miles south of Sedona on Highway 179, turn left (east) onto Morgan Road which goes through Broken Arrow Estates. Follow Morgan Road about one-half mile to its end. Here a dirt road takes off but is confused by several jeep trails. Consult your topo map and walk along what seems to be the main track. In the next one-half mile do *not* take the first two left forks but do take the third and you should be at the Devil's Dining Room.

Bewick's Wren

The Devil's Dining Room is actually a sinkhole. Sinkholes are a common topographic feature in limestone areas. Here precipitation percolated down through the Supai formation and dissolved limestone in the underlying Redwall Formation to form a cave. Then sometime later, the cave's roof of Supai collapsed, forming a hole about 75 feet deep and 25 feet across. Note the volcanic dike along one side of the hole. Near the edge grow Arizona cypress, manzanita, beargrass, mountain mahogany, cliffrose, pinyon pine, and banana yucca.

Red Rock Country Trail #11

Name: Jacks Canyon Trail (USFS #55) to Munds Mountain Trail (USFS #77)
Trailhead location: T.17N., R.6E., Sec. 35
Trailhead elevation: 4720 feet
Total vertical ascent: 1680 feet to junction of Jacks Canyon and Munds Mountain Trails
Highest point: 6400 feet on Jacks Canyon Trail
Length (one way): about 4.5 miles
Maps: 7.5' Munds Mountain; Coconino National Forest (south half)

About 6.5 miles south of Sedona on Highway 179 turn left (east) onto Jacks Canyon road. Follow it 2.7 miles until it ends at a small gate house to a private subdivision. To your right is a fence and gate. Take this road; remember to close the gate. Proceed *only* if you have a four-wheel drive vehicle to Jacks Canyon Tank, approximately 2.4 miles from the gate. Park at the tank since the jeep road only goes a few tenths of a mile farther and ends away from the trail. The trail begins about 1000 feet north of the tank on the *east* side of Jacks Canyon Wash, exactly as shown on the topo map. From here is it about 4.5 miles to the saddle between Munds Mountain and Schnebly Hill. U.S. Forest Service Trail #77 begins here and switchbacks steeply to the flat summit of Munds Mountain. The views from the saddle and summit are splendid.

Vegetation from the trailhead to the saddle includes catclaw acacia, narrowleaf yucca, one-seed juniper, snakeweed, prickly pear, pinyon pine, Arizona cypress, some singleleaf pine, mesquite, tumbleweed, shrub live oak, banana yucca, barberry, hollyleaf buckthorn, squawbush and sugar sumac. A few desert willows grow along the wash.

Gambel's Quail are common in the thick underbrush. Turkey and elk inhabit the tops of Schnebly Hill and Munds Mountain.

Between 1882 and 1884, C. M. (Jack) Montgomery, Al Doyle (famous guide and cattleman) and John Marshall constructed this trail from Montgomery's ranch in Clay Park to the Big Park area to move livestock.

Turkey

Gambel's Quail

Sugar Sumac

Scarlet Sumac

Red Rock Country Trail #12

Name: Woods Canyon Trail (Dry Beaver, USFS #93)
Trailhead location: T.16N., R.6E., Sec. 20
Trailhead elevation: 4060 feet
Total vertical ascent: 260 feet at end of trail; 1260 feet at
*   Interstate 17*
Length (one way): 3 miles to end of trail; about 14 miles to
*   Interstate 17*
Maps: 7.5" Sedona; 7.5' Munds Mountain; Coconino National
*   Forest (south half)*

Drive 8.6 miles south of Sedona on Highway 179, turn
left onto dirt road and go through the gate, closing it behind
you. Just reaching this trailhead may be an adventure. Unless
you are driving a truck or four-wheel drive vehicle, it is probably
advisable to park about one mile from Highway 179 and walk
down the road to the trailhead. This will add only about one
mile (one way) to your hike.

A Forest Service sign marks the beginning of this trail and
also the Hot Loop Trail (Red Rock Country Trail #13). The
three miles or so of trail follow Dry Beaver Creek which may
contain water in winter or spring. The water table must not be
too far below the ground's surface, though, because of the pro-
fusion of sycamore trees and an occasional cottonwood. Other
vegetation includes shrub live oak, Arizona white oak, and
other evergreen oaks (which, by the way, freely interbreed,
producing intermediate forms known as hybrids), sugar sumac,
mountain mahogany, prickly pear, catclaw acacia, mesquite,
one-seed and Utah juniper, manzanita, barberry, graythorn,
false paloverde, Mormon tea, some pinyon pine, and a few
singleleaf pine.

Singleleaf pine is very similar to the pinyon pine except
that the leaves (needles) occur singly whereas the pinyon has
two leaves per cluster or bundle.

Mormon tea and false paloverde are also sometimes confused. Mormon tea is usually a small bush, whereas false paloverde is tree-size. Also, the stems of Mormon tea are jointed
and the false paloverde stems are not. A tonic beverage may be

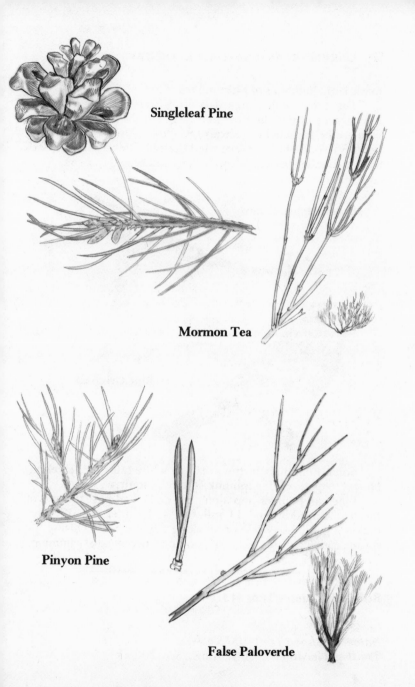

Singleleaf Pine

Mormon Tea

Pinyon Pine

False Paloverde

made from the stems of Mormon tea.

The side-blotched lizard is often seen basking on rocks. Many birds utilize the trees and large shrubs for nesting sites. Some to be expected are Shrub Jay, Plain Titmouse, Cardinal, Bell's Vireo, Bewick's Wren, Red-shafted Flicker, Gila Woodpecker, Ladder-backed Woodpecker, and Blue Grosbeak.

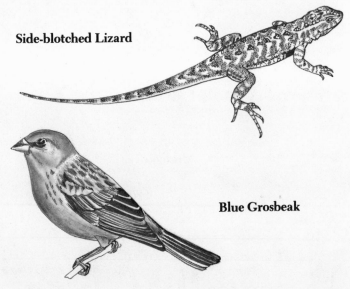

Side-blotched Lizard

Blue Grosbeak

Some mammals in the area are white-tail deer, javelina, bobcat, coyote, cliff chipmunk, and rock squirrel.

One can boulder-hop along the creek bed past the end of the trail an additional 11 miles or so to Interstate 17. This makes a good 2-day trip or one long day one-way. During the spring, running water and deep pools may necessitate swimming.

Red Rock Country Trail #13

Name: Hot Loop Trail (USFS #94)
Trailhead location: T.16N., R.6E., Sec. 20

Trailhead elevation: 4060 feet
Total vertical ascent: 1200 feet
Highest point: 5260 feet
Length (one way): about 4 miles
Maps: 7.5' Sedona; 7.5' Munds Mountain; Coconino National
Forest (south half)

This trail begins at the same location as Red Rock Country Trail #12, a nice loop walk can be done by returning on the Woods Canyon Trail. go about 1.5 miles up the Hot Loop Trail, then go southeast cross country and drop off Horse Mesa down to the Woods Canyon Trail. Round trip takes about 3 to 4 hours. If you follow the Hot Loop Trail to its end at Horse Mesa Tank, it is a much more difficult descent into Woods Canyon.

The Hot Loop Trail climbs through mainly chaparral vegetation with some influence from the desert-grassland such as false paloverde. Horse Mesa is covered by a scraggly pinyon-juniper woodland.

Watch for chunks of white Kaibab Limestone lying along the trail in contrast to the black basalt. Many of these pieces contain a speckle pattern which is fossilized sponge. To the north note the lava flow coming down the side of Lee Mountain.

Agave

Red Rock Country Trail #14

Name: Soldier Pass Trail
Trailhead location: T.17N., R.5E., Sec. 1
Trailhead elevation: 4480 feet
Total vertical ascent: 440 feet
Highest point: 4920 feet at Soldier Pass
Length (one way): 1.5 mile to Soldier Pass; 2 miles to Brins
    Mesa
Maps: 7.5' Sedona; 7.5' Wilson Mountain; Coconino National
    Forest (south half)

In West Sedona, go north on Soldier Pass road. Follow the road until it enters a clearing 1.3 miles from Highway 89A; park here. Follow any of the three roads to the right (they merge back together). In about .3 mile from the clearing the road forks, one fork going straight (take this one); the other fork goes to the right and down across the wash to Devil's Kitchen (see Red Rock Country Trail #15).

Although part of this trail has been used as a jeep road, I would recommend parking no farther than the turn-off to Devil's Kitchen. Little distance is saved by driving farther and continued use of this jeep road is only encouraging soil erosion.

It was near the mouth of Soldier Wash that officers from Camp Verde had a summer place called Camp Garden. This hike begins in an Arizona cypress woodland and ends at Soldier Pass in pinyon and juniper. Also found are manzanita, sugar sumac, false paloverde, prickly pear, and snakeweed. The diminutive pincushion cactus is common near the Pass.

About .4 mile north from the Devil's Kitchen turnoff, there are several deep potholes in the wash to the right. Water is sometimes to be found all summer in these pools and thus can become quite important to wildlife. The red-spotted toad breeds in such temporary ponds. As the water evaporates, what water remains is more easily warmed by the sun which in turn speeds up the transformation from tadpole to toad. However, should all the water evaporate before metamorphosis is completed, some tadpoles may survive by burrowing into the mud and remaining inactive until the next summer storm.

Red-spotted Toad

After another .7 mile, the trail forks again. The right fork climbs steeply, crosses some bare sandstone to finally end at three arches in the Supai Formation. These arches have formed in a large slab of rock separated from the main cliff face by a joint or fracture.

The left trail begins to ascend to Soldier Pass; two forks to the left are dead ends. Go through a fence gate and you are on top. You may continue down the other side to Dry Creek Road about 1.5 miles or follow the more obvious trail to the right (currently marked with a rock cairn) to Brins Mesa, .75 mile, for a view down Mormon Canyon to Sedona. Brins Mesa was named after an old maverick, brindled bull who ranged between Mormon Canyon and Dry Creek. Many attempted to rope him but none succeeded in capturing him. Finally two cowboys did manage to get a rope around his horns but before the bull could be pulled down, he dragged them into the cypress. It was either lose their ropes or be battered against the trees. Instead, they shot the old bull dead.

Red Rock Country Trail #15

Name: Devil's Kitchen Trail
Trailhead location: T.17N., R.5E., Sec. 1
Trailhead elevation: 4480 feet

Total vertical ascent: negligible
Highest point: 4480 feet
Length (one way): .4 mile
Maps: 7.5' Wilson Mountain; Coconino National Forest
(south half)

Follow road directions given in Red Rock Country Trail #14. Like the Devil's Dining Room (Red Rock Country Trail #10), this is another collapsed cave or sinkhole. People were living in the area in the 1880's when the roof fell in. It reportedly sounded like a mammoth explosion and dust darkened the sky all day. The sinkhole is 65 feet deep and 112 feet across. Around the edge of the hole grow manzanita, shrub live oak, Arizona cypress, agave, and buckbrush.

Manzanita

Red Rock Country Trail #16

Name: Devil's Bridge Trail (USFS #120)
Trailhead location: T.18N., R.5E., Sec. 35
Trailhead elevation: 4600 feet
Total vertical ascent: 320 feet

Highest point: 4920 feet
Length (one way): .4 mile
Maps: 7.5' Wilson Mountain; Coconino National Forest
    (south half)

Follow Road Log #4 to Sterling Canyon Road. Follow Sterling Canyon Road another 1.2 miles and there is a fork to the right. Take this road to its end, approximately .4 mile.

The Devil's Bridge Trail begins immediately to the south of the turn-around parking area. The trail is steep but short and in good condition, having been improved by the Civilian Conservation Corps in the 1930's.

This is another natural bridge in the Supai Formation. A slab of sandstone was separated from the main wall by a joint or fracture. Erosion was then able to attack not only the front of the slab but also the newly exposed back surface. This "double action" finally weathered a hole through the slab which gradually became larger to form the bridge we see today.

From the bridge is a terrific view north and west of the Dry Creek drainage basin. Beautiful towers of Supai and Coconino Sandstone loom in the distance.

Red Rock Country Trail #17

Name: Vultee Arch Trail (USFS #22)
Trailhead location: T.18N., R.5E., Sec. 13
Trailhead elevation 4800 feet
Total vertical ascent: 440 feet
Highest point: 5240 feet
Length (one way): 2 miles
Maps: 7.5' Wilson Mountain; Coconino National Forest
    (south half)

Follow the road description given for Red Rock Country Trail #16 as far as the fork to Devil's Bridge. Instead of turning off, continue on Forest Service Road 152C to its end at the mouth of Sterling Canyon. A small wood sign marks the trailhead.

The trail gradually climbs through Arizona cypress, manzanita, silk-tassel bush, alligator-bark juniper, and agave. Scrub Jays, Plain Titmice, Bewick's Wrens, and Blue-gray Gnatcatchers may be seen or heard.

At the end of the trail look toward the north to see the arch which is made of Supai Sandstone. Vultee Arch was named after aircraft designer Gerard F. Vultee. He and his wife Sylvia were killed 29 January 1938 when their plane crashed on East Pocket Mesa during a snowstorm.

Supposedly an ancient Indian trail once continued up Sterling Canyon to its head, then up and over and down to the Indian Gardens area. This would have, of course, provided quicker access to Oak Creek from Upper Dry Creek than having to go south around Wilson Mountain.

Plain Titmouse

Blue-gray Gnatcatcher

Red Rock Country Trail #18

Name: Dry Creek Pack Trail
Trailhead location: T.18N., R.5E., Sec. 13
Trailhead elevation: 4800 feet
Total vertical ascent: 200 feet
Highest point: about 5000 feet at end of trail
Length (one way): 1.5 miles
Maps: 7.5' Wilson Mountain;Coconino National Forest (south
*   half)*

To find this trailhead follow the directions in Road Log #4 to Sterling Canyon Road. Then follow Sterling Canyon to the Vultee Arch trailhead (Red Rock Country Trail #17). Just before reaching the Vultee Arch trailhead, a primitive jeep track takes off to the north. Park and follow this on foot across Sterling Canyon Wash, go to Dry Creek Wash, follow the main cow path northward, watch for the crossing of Dry Creek Wash .2 of a mile or so from your vehicle. Once on the left (west) side of the wash, numerous rock cairns mark the trail. The trail shown on the topographic map just peters out after about 1.5 miles. However, Dry Creek and the many side canyons are long and wild. An aggressive bushwacker can spend many days getting to know this maze of canyons.

During spring, running water may be encountered, simplifying extended trips.

The vegetation is varied and lush. Species from all eight of the major communities can be seen here. Cottonwood, sycamore, Douglas fir, ponderosa pine, and Arizona cypress can be seen growing side by side. The Supai has formed little grottos which harbor a variety of ferns, monkeyflowers, columbine, and mosses.

The remoteness of this section of the Red Rock Country is exemplified by the existence of mountain lions. The presence of this shy creature is usually only known through tracks left in the soft dirt by the washes. Little is known about the life history and ecology of the lion in Arizona. At one time it was thought that a predator such as the lion took a heavy toll on deer and other prey animals. Thus, lions were hunted relentlessly. Deer populations soared and the range became so overgrazed that deer began to die of starvation. Today, in most places, it is realized that predators are a necessary part of the ecosystem. Not only do predators help in limiting prey populations, but their hunting activities keep grazing animals on the move and prevents overgrazing of any particular area.

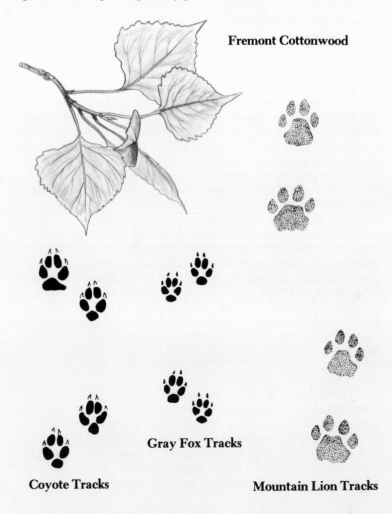

Fremont Cottonwood

Gray Fox Tracks

Coyote Tracks

Mountain Lion Tracks

Red Rock Country Trail #19

Name: Secret Canyon Trail
Trailhead location: T.18N., R.5E., Sec. 23
Trailhead elevation 4680 feet
Total vertical ascent: 240 feet
Highest point: 4920 feet
Length (one way): 3 miles
Maps: 7.5' Wilson Mountain; Coconino National Forest
(south half)

Follow road directions in Road Log #4 to get on Forest Service Road #152C, the Sterling Canyon Road. About 3.5 miles from the junction of Forest Service Road #152C with #152, a poor jeep track takes off to the left and crosses Dry Creek. The crossing is very rocky and hazardous. It is best to park your vehicle and walk.

The trail is easy to follow for about 2.5 miles as it travels along Secret Canyon Wash, which in spring may have water. The last half mile of trail is followed by careful attention to blazes on trees. Then the trail just ends for no apparent reason.

Instead of following the last one-half mile it is more interesting to follow the main drainage of Secret Canyon. the bushwacker can really get into some scenic and primitive country. Several black bear live in the area along with lion, deer, cliff chipmunks, and other typical chaparral and woodland species.

Black Bear

The botany at the trailhead is mostly Arizona Cypress, sycamore, cottonwood, and manzanita. Near the trail's end there is more one-seed juniper, agave, silk-tassel bush, ponderosa pine, pinyon pine, evergreen oak, and catclaw acacia.

Allegedly, a group of polygamous Mormons hid out in Secret Canyon in the 1880's. The Edmunds-Tucker Law of 1882 had made such a life style "unlawful cohabitation" and many Mormon families fled to secluded canyons.

Red Rock Country Trail #20

Name: Long Canyon Trail
Trailhead location: T.18N., R.5E., Sec. 21
Trailhead elevation: 4560 feet
Total vertical ascent: 440 feet
Highest point: 5000 feet
Length (one way): 2.2 miles
Maps: 7.5' Wilson Mountain; Coconino National Forest (south
*   half); foot trail not shown beyond jeep road*

Follow Road Log #4 to the Long Canyon Road. One mile down Long Canyon Road and just before a cattleguard, turn left on to a jeep track and park. Walk along the jeep trail, taking the right fork at about one-half mile from your vehicle. Another half mile and the jeep road becomes a foot trail. By hiking 1.25 miles farther, the trail ends at a Supai cliff on the right (north). Scattered through the area are small Indian ruins. These were probably built by the Sinagua sometime between A.D. 1125 and A.D. 1300. There are a few pictographs or drawings. Please do not touch or disturb them.

Along the trail are some outstanding groves of Arizona cypress. Take a closs look at the bark on some of the smaller trees. Note the thin scales of bark, peeling off to reveal a beautiful dark red inner bark. In the southern portion of the United States, this tree is grown for use as christmas trees. The wood of Arizona cypress is used occasionally for fence posts, but it is too scarce to be lumbered.

Long Canyon contains towering cliffs, spires, little arches and natural windows, and dark secluded alcoves. Cross-country hiking is somewhat limited because of thick chaparral vegetation.

Common birds include the Raven, Bewick's Wren, Plain Titmouse, Scrub Jay, and Black-throated Sparrow.

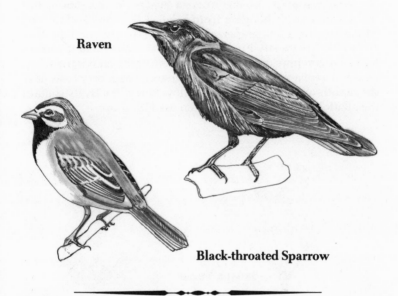

Raven

Black-throated Sparrow

Red Rock Country Trail #21

Name: Fay Canyon Arch Trail
Trailhead location: T.18N., R.5E., Sec. 32
Trailhead elevation: 4600 feet
Total vertical ascent: 240 feet
Highest point: 4840 feet
Length (one way): .8 mile
Maps: 7.5' Wilson Mountain; Coconino National Forest
      (south half)

Follow Road Log #4 to mileage 8.2, turn off to Fay Canyon. Park in the clearing.

Walk up the jeep road about one-half mile, keeping an eye on the right (northeast) cliff face. The arch looks like a deep overhang instead of an arch. There is a short steep trail to the arch itself. There is a small Sinagua dwelling under the arch dating from approximately the 12th or 13th century.

Besides evergreen oaks, Arizona cypress, manzanita, notice the Arizona grape hanging from some of the trees and bushes. Also, there are a few singleleaf pinyons in the canyon. The very large oaks are mostly Emory oak. Other plants include squaw-bush, pinyon pine, one-seed juniper, barberry, and narrowleaf yucca. There are a few clumps of western soapberry trees near the mouth of Fay Canyon. the yellow berry-like fruits contain the alkaloid saponin and have been used for soap.

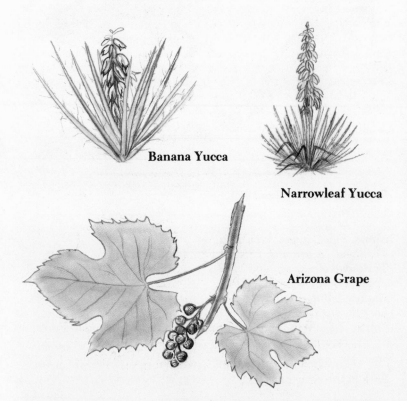

Banana Yucca

Narrowleaf Yucca

Arizona Grape

Red Rock Trail #22

Name: Loy Canyon Trail (USFS #5)
Trailhead location: T.18N., R.4E., Sec. 22
Trailhead elevation: 4720 feet
Total vertical ascent: 1680 feet to intersection of Loy Canyon
      Trail and Secret Mountain Trail
Highest point: 6400 feet on Loy Canyon Trail
Length (one way): 5 miles to intersection with the Secret
      Mountain Trail
Maps: 7.5' Loy Butte; Coconino National Forest (north and
      south halves); trailhead location shown incorrectly on
      both maps

To find the trailhead, drive 9.9 miles west of Sedona on Highway 89A. Turn right on to Forest Service Road #525; at mile 2.7 take right fork; at mile 5.7 take left; sign says Loy Butte - 4 miles. At mile 9.2, just before crossing a wash, is a small wooden Forest Service sign marking the Loy Canyon Trail.

The trail begins by following the fence. As the trail turns back toward Loy Canyon Wash and passes a private ranch, it becomes confused by livestock paths. Just keep heading up the wash. About .2 of a mile beyond the ranch buildings you should be able to locate a fairly definite trail running parallel to the wash as shown on the topo map.

The first four miles have a gentle grade and go through a mixture of pinyon-juniper woodland with a thick understory of chaparral and desert-grassland species. The presence of catclaw acacia may dictate the wearing of long pants even on a hot day. Evergreen oaks are prevalent.

During the last steep mile or so, ponderosa pine comes in. On the forest floor you may notice Oregon grape, a low creeping shrub often mistaken for holly. Its berries make a delightful jelly and are also eaten by wildlife. The roots produce a brilliant yellow dye, and some Indians use a decoction of the leaves to treat rheumatism.

The last half-mile switchbacks up to the rim and offers some fine views. At the rim Loy Canyon Trail intersects with Secret Mountain Trail, USFS #109, which meanders about

Oregon Grape

five miles, offering spectacular vistas. Several other trails (such as USFS #114) branch off and lead to other rim points on Secret Mountain. This rugged, remote area of Arizona has been referred to as the haunted wilderness. Several legends claim that lost Spanish mines and ghosts of lost hunters exist in the area. During the late 1800's, the region was used by outlaws as a hideout. Rumor has it that the "Phantom Band" or horse-rustlers had a more or less permanent camp here. Stolen horses were brought there, brands cleverly changed, then the horses were taken to Utah, Colorado, or even New Mexico to be sold.

Samuel Loy and his son James built a log cabin up in Loy Canyon in the 1870's. However, during a drouth in the 1880's, their water source dried up and they were forced to move to Oak Creek.

Long before the settlers arrived, the Sinagua and then later the Yavapai-Apache also lived in the area.

Red Rock Country Trail #23

Name: Mooney Trail (USFS #12)
Trailhead location: T.18N., R.4E., Sec. 16
Trailhead elevation: 4920 feet
Total vertical ascent: 1400 feet
Highest point: 6320 feet
Length (one way): 4.5 miles
Maps: 7.5' Loy Butte; Coconino National Forest (north and
*   south halves)*

Drive 9.9 miles west of Sedona on Highway 89A. Turn right on to Forest Service Road #525. Check odometer and at mile 2.7 take left fork. This is Forest Service Road #525C. At about mile 8.5 turn right, go through gate (please close), go past Black Tank and keep to the left at any other division in the road. You will need 4-wheel drive to reach the trailhead by vehicle. Otherwide, park and walk. Near the end of the jeep road the yucca-like plants with the very long narrow leaves are beargrass. At the road's end do not follow the vague foot trail leading uphill as shown on the topo map. The trail here is overgrown; instead, walk northeast and down cross-country. In about 150 to 300 feet you will meet a cow path heading up canyon. This is it. You may need to consult the map often to stay with the trail. This one was built in the 1870's to move livestock on and off the rim country.

Do not be surprised if you run into a small herd of javelina, sometimes called peccaries. Although farther north than what most field guides show as their normal distribution, javelina nevertheless do occur along the Mogollon Rim. They seem to like the thick chaparral for cover and the ubiquitous prickly pear is probably their favorite food. The javelina have received an unfair reputation as being fierce fighters, attacking humans wantonly. True, when cornered, the little pig may put up quite a battle. However, the javelina's supposed charge at people is most likely the result of its poor eyesight and fear-induced confusion.

About one-half mile before beginning to switchback up to Buck Ridge, the trail crosses the dry creek from east to west.

Here there is a beautiful grotto and arch in the Supai Formation.

The name Mooney may have come from a pioneer stockman who supposedly camped nearby. Another possibility is that it has some connection with prospector Daniel W. Mooney, who fell to his death while attempting to descend a cliff in the Grand Canyon.

Red Rock Country Trail #24

Name: Casner Mountain Trail (USFS #8)
Trailhead location: T.18N., R.4E., Sec. 30
Trailhead elevation: 4760 feet
Total vertical ascent: 2076 feet
Highest point: 6836 feet
Length (one way): 7 miles
Maps: 7.5' Loy Butte; Coconino National Forest (north and south halves)

Follow the road directions for Red Rock Country Trail #23, except do not turn off at Black Tank. Instead, proceed toward Sycamore Pass. Where the road passes under the power transmission lines, pull off and park. Follow the power line uphill and you will shortly come to a poor jeep trail. This is Casner Mountain Trail, named after George R. Casner, who pastured sheep here about 1900.

It is a hard pull up to the top of Casner Mountain, but after that the trail levels out considerably. The spectacular views of the San Francisco Peaks, Sycamore Canyon Wilderness Area, the Verde Valley, and the Red Rock Country make the effort worth it.

A nice loop trail can be done by connecting with the Mooney Trail, Red Rock Country Trail #23.

THE CHECKLISTS

The following section contains checklists of the known vascular plants and vertebrate animals of the Oak Creek Canyon-Red Rock Country. It should be emphasized that because of the dynamic quality of living organisms checklists are destined to be incomplete. Changing environmental conditions, human-related influence, and quirks of nature not yet understood determine the abundance and specific distribution of plants and animals from year to year. Yet checklists can be interesting and useful indicators of what was present at a particular point in time.

These checklists also contain the scientific name for each plant and animal. This is very important for anyone concerned with the proper identification of these organisms. Many plants and animals have numerous common names which are determined by local usage. However, there is only one scientific name for each organism so confusion is minimized.

A checklist of non-vascular plants can be found in A. B. Johnsen's *The Bryophytes and Lichens of West Fork, Oak Creek Canyon*, Plateau, 36(2) :54-62.

Lists of aquatic insects appear in *An Examination of the Aquatic Insect Populations of Oak Creek, Arizona* by Eric B. May, 1972, unpublished master's thesis, Northern Arizona University and *A Season Analysis of Aquatic Insect Populations in Oak Creek, Arizona*, by J. F. Parrott, 1975, unpublished master's thesis, Northern Arizona University.

The abundance terms used in the vertebrate checklists are defined as follows:

Common: Almost always seen by a trained observer during proper season in appropriate habitat.

Uncommon: Occassionaly seen but not a surprise to trained observers.

Rare: Always a surprise when encountered but not out of normal range.

Irregular: Densities vary widely from year to year.

Hypothetical: Within normal geographic range and to be expected but not yet encountered.

OAK CREEK CANYON-RED ROCK COUNTRY
VASCULAR PLANT CHECKLIST

Scientific names conform with W.B. McDougall's *Seed Plants of Northern Arizona*, 1973, Northern Arizona Society of Science and Art, Inc., Flagstaff. Family numbers correspond to those used in Kearney and Peebles' *Arizona Flora*, University of California Press, 1969.

1. **SELAGINELLACEAE** — Selaginella Family
   Selaginella underwoodii - Little Club Moss
3. **EQUISETACEAE** — Horsetail Family
   Equisetum arvense - Horsetail
   Equisetum hiemale - Scouring Rush
   Equisetum laevigatum - Scouring Rush
6. **MARSILEACEAE** — Pepperwort Family
   Marsilea mucronata - Pepperwort
7. **POLYPODIACEAE** — Fern Family
   Adiantum capillus-veneris - Venushair Fern
   Adiantum pedatum - Maidenhair Fern
   Asplenium trichomanes - Spleenwort
   Cheilanthes covillei - Lip Fern
   Cheilanthes feei - Lip Fern
   Cheilanthes fendleri - Brittle Fern
   Cystopteris bulbifera - Bladder Fern
   Cystopteris fragilis - Bladder Fern
   Dryopteris filix-mas - Male Fern
   Pellaea atropurpurea - Cliff-brake
   Pellaea longimucronata - Cliff-brake
   Polypodium vulgare - Polypody
   Polystichum lonchitis - Holly Fern
   Pteridium aquilinum var. *pubescens* - Bracken Fern
   Woodsia mexicana
   Woodsia oregana
8. **PINACEAE** — Pine Family
   Abies concolor - White Fir
   Abies lasiocarpa - Alpine Fir
   Picea engelmannii - Engelmann Spruce
   Picea pungens - Blue Spruce

Pinus edulis - Pinyon Pine
Pinus monophylla - Singleleaf Pine
Pinus ponderosa - Ponderosa Pine
Pseudotsuga menziesii - Douglas Fir

9. CUPRESSACEAE — Cypress Family
Cupressus arizonica - Arizona Cypress
Juniperus deppeana - Alligator-bark Juniper
Juniperus monosperma - One-seed Juniper
Juniperus osteosperma - Utah Juniper
Juniperus scopulorum - Rocky Mountain Juniper

10. EPHEDRACEAE — Joint Fir Family
Ephedra viridis - Mormon Tea or Joint Fir

11. TYPHACEAE — Cattail Family
Typha domingensis - Cattail
Typha latifolia - Broadleaf Cattail

18. GRAMINEAE — Grass Family
Agropyron desertorum - Wheat Grass
Agropyron subsecundum - Wheat Grass
Agropyron trachycaulum - Wheat Grass
Agrostis alba - Bent Grass
Agrostis exarata - Bent Grass
Alopecurus aequalis - Foxtail
Alopecurus carolinianus - Foxtail
Andropogon hallii - Bluestem
Aristida fendleriana - Fendler Three Awn
Aristida glauca - Three Awn
Aristida purpurea - Purple Three Awn
Aristida ternipes var. *minor* - Spider Grass
Bouteloua barbata - Six-weeks Grama
Bouteloua curtipendula - Sideoats Grama
Bouteloua eriopoda - Black Grama
Bouteloua hirsuta - Hairy Grama
Bromus inermus - Smooth Brome
Bromus richardsonii - Fringed Brome
Bromus rigidus - Rip Gut Grass
Bromus rubens - Red Brome
Bromus tectorum - Cheat
Bromus trinii - Chilean Chess
Cenchrus pauciflorus - Field Sandbur

Cynodon dactylon - Bermuda Grass
Dactylis glomerata - Orchard Grass
Digitaria sanguinalis - Crabgrass
Echinochloa crusgalli - Barnyard Grass
Elymus canadensis - Canadian Wild Rye
Elymus glaucus - Wild Rye
Eragrostis cilianensis - Stinkgrass
Eragrostis diffusa - Spreading Love Grass
Eragrostis intermedia - Plains Love Grass
Eragrostis mexicana - Mexican Love Grass
Glyceria striata - Fowl Manna Grass
Hilaria jamesii - Galleta
Hilaria mutica - Tobosa
Holcus lanatus - Velvet Grass
Hordeum jubatum - Foxtail Barley
Koeleria cristata - Mountain June Grass
Lolium perenne - Perennial Ryegrass
Melica porteri - Melica
Muhlenbergia emersleyi -Bull Grass
Muhlenbergia polycaulis - Muhly
Muhlenbergia racemosa - Muhly
Muhlenbergia sinuata - Muhly
Oryzopsis hymenoides - Indian Rice Grass
Panicum bulbosum - Panic Grass
Panicum capillare - Old Witch Grass
Panicum hallii - Hall's Panicum
Panicum scribnerianum - Panic Grass
Phalaris canariensis - Canary Grass
Phleum pratense - Timothy Grass
Poe bigelovii - Blue Grass
Poa fendleriana - Mutton Grass
Setaria lutescens - Yellow Bristlegrass
Setaria viridis - Green Bristlegrass
Sitanion longifolium - Squirreltail
Sorghum halepense - Johnson Grass
Sporobolus airoides - Alkali Sacaton
Sporobolus cryptandrus - Sand dropseed
Stipa comata - Needle and Thread Grass
Tridens pilosus - Hairy Tridens
Tridens pulchellus - Fluff Grass

19. **CYPERACEAE** — Sedge Family
    Carex geophila - Sedge
    Carex occidentalis - Sedge
    Carex senta - River Sedge
    Cyperus fendlerianus - Flat Sedge
    Scirpus microcarpus - Bulrush

24. **COMMELINACEAE** — Spiderwort Family
    Commelina dianthifolia - Day Flower
    Tradescantia occidentalis - Spiderwort
    Tradescantia pinetorum - Spiderwort

26. **JUNCACEAE** — Rush Family
    Juncus interior - Rush
    juncus longistylis - Rush
    Juncus saximontanus - Rush
    Juncus tenuis - Rush

27. **LILIACEAE** — Lily Family
    Allium bigelovii - Wild Onion
    Allium geyeri - Wild Onion
    Allium palmeri - Wild Onion
    Asparagus officinale - Asparagus
    Calochortus ambiguus - Mariposa
    Dichelostemma pulchellum - Bluedicks
    Disporum trachycarpum - Fairybells
    Fritillaria atropurpurea - Fritillary
    Nolina microcarpa - Beargrass
    Smilicina racemosa - False Solomon-seal
    Smilicina stellata - Star Flower
    Triteleia lemmonae
    Yucca angustissima - Narrowleaf Yucca
    Yucca baccata - Banana Yucca
    Yucca elata - Soaptree Yucca
    Zigadenus elagans - Death Camas

28. **AMARYLLIDACEAE** — Amaryllis Family
    Agave parryi - Century Plant, Agave

29. **IRIDACEAE** — Iris Family
    Iris missouriensis - Iris

30. **ORCHIDACEAE** — Orchid Family
    Corallorhiza maculata - Coralroot
    Epipactis gigantea - Helleborine

Goodyera oblongifolia - Rattlesnake plantain
Habenaria sparsiflora - Rein Orchid

32. SALICACEAE — Willow Family
Populus acuminata - Lanceleaf Cottonwood
Populus augustifolia - Narrowleaf Cottonwood
Populus fremontii - Fremont Cottonwood
Populus tremuloides - Quaking Aspen
Salix gooddingii - Goodding Willow
Salix laevigata - Red Willow
Salix lasiolepis - Arroyo Willow

33. JUGLANDACEAE — Walnut Family
Juglans major - Arizona Walnut

34. BETULACEAE — Birch Family
Alnus oblongifolia - New Mexico Alder, Arizona Alder
Ostrya knowltoni - Hophornbeam

35. FAGACEAE — Beech Family
Quercus arizonica - Arizona White Oak
Quercus chrysolepis - Canyon Live Oak
Quercus dunnii - Palmer Oak
Quercus emoryi - Emory Oak
Quercus gambelii - Gambel's Oak
Quercus grisea - Gray Oak
Quercus reticulata - Netleaf Oak
Quercus turbinella - Shrub Live Oak
Quercus undulata - Wavyleaf oak
Quercus turbinella x *Q. arizonica*

36. ULMACEAE — Elm Family
Celtis reticulata - Netleaf Hackberry

37. MORACEAE — Mulberry Family
Humulus americanus - Hop
Morus microphylla - Mulberry

39. LORANTHACEAE — Mistletoe Family
Arceuthobium vaginatum - Small Mistletoe
  (on Ponderosa Pine)
Phoradendron boleanum - Mistletoe (on Juniper
  and Cypress)
Phoradendron coryae - Mistletoe (on Oak)
Phoradendron flavescens - Mistletoe (on Cottonwood
  and Sycamore)

40. SANTALACEAE — Sandalwood family
   Comandra pallida - Bastard Toadflax
43. POLYGONACEAE — Buckwheat Family
   Eriogonum abertianum - Wild Buckwheat
   Eriogonum alatum - Winged Eriogonum
   Eriogonum aureum
   Eriogonum corymbosum - Wild Buckwheat
   Eriogonum jamesii
   Eriogonum pharnaceoides - Wild Buckwheat
   Eriogonum polycladon - Sorrel Erigonum
   Eriogonum umbellatum - Sulfur Flower
   Eriogonum vimineum - Broom Eriogonum
   Eriogonum wrightii - Wild Buckwheat
   Polygonum aviculare - Knotweed
   Polygonum convolvulus - Climbing Buckwheat
   Polygonum lapathifolium - Smartweed
   Polygonum persicaria - Smartweed
   Rumex altissimus - Dock
   Rumex crispus - Curley-leaf Dock
   Rumex hymenosepalus - Canaigre, Wild Rhubarb
44. CHENOPODIACEAE — Goose Foot Family
   Atriplex canescens -Four-wing Saltbush
   Chenopodium album - Lambs Quarters
   Salsola kali - Russian-thistle, Tumbleweed
45. AMARANTHACEAE — Amaranth Family
   Amaranthus albus - Amaranth
   Amaranthus palmeri - Amaranth
46. NYCTAGINACEAE — Four-o'clock Family
   Allionia incarnata - Trailing Four-o'clock
   Mirabilis multiflora - Four-o'clock
   Oxybaphus linearis
   Tripterocalyx wootonii - Tripterocalyx
49. PORTULACACEAE — Portulaca Family
   Claytonia lanceolata - Spring Beauty
   Lewisia brachycalyx
   Montia perfoliata - Miner's Lettuce
50. CARYOPHYLLACEAE — Pink Family
   Cerastium texanum - Chickweed
   Silene antirrhina - Sleepy Catchfly

Silene laciniata - Mexican Campion
Silene scouleri - Scouler's Catchfly
Stellaria jamesiana - Starwort

52. RANUNCULACEAE — Crowfoot Family

Aconitum columbianum - Monkshood
Anemone cylindrica - Anemone
Anemone tuberosa
Aquilegia chrysantha - Golden Columbine
Cimicifuga arizonica - Bugbane
Clematis ligusticifolia - Clematis
Delphinium geranifolium - Larkspur
Delphinium scaposum - Delphinium
Myosurus aristatus - Mouse-tail
Ranunculus aquatilis
Ranunculus cymbalaria - Desert Crowfoot
Ranunculus inamoenus - Buttercup
Ranunculus oreogenes - Collom's Buttercup
Ranunculus testiculatus
Thalictrum fendleri - Meadow Rue

53. BERBERIDACEAE — Barberry Family

Berberis haematocarpa - Red Mahonia, Barberry
Berberis repens - Creeping Mahonia, Oregon Grape

55. PAPAVERACEAE — Poppy Family

Argemone pleiacantha - Prickly Poppy
Corydalis aurea - Golden Corydal
Eschscholtzia mexicana - Mexican Poppy
Platystemon californicus - Creamcups

56. CRUCIFERAE — Mustard Family

Arabis glabra
Arabis perennans - Rock Cress
Capsella bursa-pastoris - Shepherd's Purse
Chorispora tenella
Descurainia obtusa - Tansy Mustard
Descurainia pinnata - Tansy Mustard
Draba asprella - Draba
Draba cuneifolia
Erysimum capitatum - Western Wallflower
Erysimum repandum
Lepidium densiflorum - Peppergrass

Lesquerella cinerea
Lesquerella gordonii - Gordon's Bladderpod
Rorippa nasturtium-aquaticum - Watercress
Sisymbrium linearifolium - Sisymbrium Mustard
Streptanthus cordatus - Twist Flower
Thelypodium wrightii
Thlaspi fendleri - Wild Candytuft

57. CAPPARIDACEAE — Caper Family

Cleome jonesii - Yellow Beeplant
Cleome serrulata - Rocky Mountain Beeplant

60. SAXIFRAGACEAE — Saxifrage Family

Fendlera rupicola - Fendler bush
Heuchera eastwoodiae
Heuchera novomexicana
Heuchera parvifolia - Alum-root
Heuchera versicolor
Lithophragma tenellam - Woodland Star
Parnassia parviflora - Grass of Parnassus
Philadelphus microphyllus - Mock Orange
Ribes cereum - Wax Currant
Ribes pinetorum - Orange Gooseberry
Saxifraga rhomboidea - Saxifrage

61. PLATANACEAE — Plane-tree Family

Platanus wrightii - Sycamore

63. ROSACEAE — Rose Family

Agrimonia gryposepala - Agrimony
Amelanchier utahensis - Serviceberry
Cercocarpus montanus - Mountain Mahogany
Chamaebatiaria millefolium - Fernbush
Cowania mexicana - Cliffrose
Crataegus erythropoda - Hawthorn
Fragaria ovalis - Strawberry
Geum triflorum - Oldman whisker
Holodiscus dumosus - Rock-spiraea
Petrophytum caespitosum - Rock-mat
Potentilla glandulosa - Cinquefoil
Potentilla thurberi - Red Cinquefoil
Prunus emarginata - Bitter Cherry
Prunus serotina ssp. *virens* - Chokecherry

Prunus virginiana - Common chokecherry
Rosa arizonica - Arizona Rose
Rubus leucodermis -Western Black Raspberry
Rubus neomexicanus - New Mexican Raspberry
Rubus procerus - Himalaya Berry, Blackberry

64. LEGUMINOSAE — Pea Family

Acacia greggii - Catclaw Acacia
Astragalus calycosus - Milkvetch
Astragalus lentiginosus - Loco Weed
Astragalus tephrodes
Astragalus troglodytus
Cassia bauhinioides - Senna
Dalea albiflora - Pea-bush
Dalea formosa - Indigo Bush
Desmodium grahamii - Tick Clover
Krameria parvifolia - Range Ratany
Lathyrus arizonicus - Arizona Peavine
Lathyrus leucanthus - Aspen Peavine
Lotus humistratus
Lotus mearnsii
Lotus wrightii - Deer Vetch
Lupinus hillii - Hill's Lupine
Lupinus kingii
Lupinus palmeri - Palmer Lupine
Medicago lupulina - Black Medick
Medicago sativa - Alfalfa
Melilotus alba - White Sweet Clover
Melilotus officinalis - Yellow Sweet Clover
Mimosa buincifera - Wait-a-minute
Petalostemum searlsiae - Prairie Clover
Phaseolus angustissimus - Bean
Prosopis juliflora - Mesquite
Psoralea tenuiflora - Scurf Pea
Robinia neomexicana - New Mexico Locust
Thermopsis pinetorum - Golden Pea
Trifolium rusbyi - Rusby Clover
Vicia americana - Vetch

65. GERANIACEAE — Geranium Family

Erodium cicutarium - Filaree
Erodium texanum - Heron Bill

Geranium caespitosum - Crane's Bill
Geranium fremontii
Geranium parryi
Geranium richardsonii - White Crane's Bill

66. **OXALIDACEAE** — Wood-sorrel Family
Oxalis metcalfei - Wood-sorrel

68. **ZYGOPHYLLACEAE** — Caltrop Family
Larrea tridentata - Creosote Bush

69. **RUTACEAE** — Rue Family
Ptelea angustifolia - Narrowleaf Hoptree
Ptelea pallida - Hoptree
Thamnosma texana

70. **SIMARUBACEAE** — Ailanthus Family
Ailanthus altissima - Tree-of-Heaven

73. **POLYGALACEAE** — Milkwort Family
Polygala scoparioides - Milkwort

74. **EUPHORBIACEAE** — Spurge Family
Croton texensis - Dove Weed
Euphorbia albomarginata - Rattlesnake Weed
Euphorbia fendleri
Euphorbia lurida - Spurge
Euphorbia serpyllifolia
Tragia stylaris - Nose-burn

76. **BUXACEAE** — Boxwood Family
Simondsia chinensis - Jojoba, Goat-nut

77. **ANACARDIACEAE** — Cashew Family
Rhus glabra - Scarlet Sumac
Rhus ovata - Sugar Sumac
Rhus radicans - Poison Ivy
Rhus trilobata - Squawbush

78. **CELASTRACEAE** — Bittersweet Family
Canotia holacantha - False Paloverde, Canotia
Forsellesia nevadensis - Greasebush
Pachystima myrsinites - Myrtle Boxleaf

79. **ACERACEAE** — Maple Family
Acer grandidentatum - Bigtooth Maple
Acer negundo - Box Elder

80. **SAPINDACEAE** — Soapberry Family
Sapindus saponaria - Soapberry

81. RHAMNACEAE — Buckthorn Family
 Ceanothus fendleri - Fendler's Buckbrush
 Ceanothus greggii - Gregg's Buckbrush
 Ceanothus integerrimus - Deerbrush
 Condalia lycioides - Graythorn
 Rhamnus betulaefolia - Birchleaf Buckthorn
 Rhamnus californica - Coffeeberry
 Rhamnus crocea - Redberry Buckthorn, Hollyleaf
  Buckthorn

82. VITACEAE — Grape Family
 Parthenocissus inserta - Virginia Creeper
 Vitis arizonica - Grape

84. MALVACEAE — Mallow Family
 Abutilon parvulum-Indian Mallow
 Althaea rosea - Hollyhock
 Sidalcea neomexicana - Checker Mallow
 Sphaeralcea fendleri - Globe Mallow
 Sphaeralcea grossulariaefolia - Globe Mallow
 Sphaeralcea parvifolia - Globe Mallow
 Sphaeralcea rusbyi - Globe Mallow

86. HYPERICACEAE — St. Johnswort Family
 Hypericum formosum - St. Johnswort

88. TAMARICACEAE — Tamarix Family
 Tamarix pentandra (= chinensis) - Salt Cedar

91. VIOLACEAE — Violet Family
 Hybanthus verticillatus - Green-violet
 Viola adunca - Violet
 Viola canadensis - White Violet
 Viola nephrophylla - Wanderer Violet

93. LOASACEAE — Loasa Family
 Mentzelia albicaulis - Stickleaf
 Mentzelia pumila - Stickleaf

94. CACTACEAE — Cactus Family
 Enchinocereus fasciculatus - Hedgehog
 Mamillaria sp. - Pincushion
 Opuntia leptocaulis - Cholla
 Opuntia macrorhiza - Prickly Pear
 Opuntia phaeacantha - Prickly Pear
 Opuntia whipplei - Cholla

97. ONAGRACEAE — Evening Primrose Family
   Circaea alpina
   Epilobium adenocaulon - Sticky Willow-weed
   Gaura gracilis
   Oenothera albicaulis - Evening Primrose
   Oenothera caespitosa - Evening Primrose
   Oenothera hookeri - Evening Primrose
   Oenothera laciniata - Evening Primrose
   Oenothera neomexicana - Evening Primrose
   Oenothera procera
   Oenothera runcinata
   Zauschneria californica - Hummingbird Trumpet

99. ARALLIACEAE — Ginseng Family
   Aralia racemosa

100. UMBELLIFERAE — Carrot Family
   Aletes macdougalli
   Conium maculatum - Poison Hemlock
   Cymopterus multinervatus
   Daucus pusillus - Carrot
   Ligusticum porteri - Chuckupate
   Lomatium dissectum - Biscuit root
   Lomatium macdougalli - Macdougal Indian Root
   Lomatium nevadense - Indian Root
   Osmorhiza chilensis - Sweetroot
   Osmorhiza depauperata - Sweetroot
   Pastinaca sativa - Parsnip
   Perideria parishii - Wild Caroway
   Pseudocymopterus montanus

101. CORNACEAE — Dogwood Family
   Cornus stolonifera - American Dogwood
   Garrya flavescens - Silk-tassel Bush
   Garrya wrightii - Silk-tassel Bush

103. ERICACEAE — Heather Family
   Arctostaphylos pringlei - Yellow-leaf Manzanita
   Arctostaphylos pungens - Point-leaf Manzanita
   Chimaphila umbellata - Pipsissewa

104. PRIMULACEAE — Primrose Family
   Androsace septentrionalis - Rock Jasmine
   Lysimachia ciliata - Loose-stripe

106. FOUQUIERIACEAE — Ocotillo Family
　　Fouquieria splendens - Ocotillo, Coach-whip
108. OLEACEAE — Olive Family
　　Forestiera neomexicana - Desert Olive
　　Fraxinus anomala - Singleleaf Ash
　　Fraxinus pennsylvanica - Velvet Ash
　　Menadora scabra
110. GENTIANACEAE — Gentian Family
　　Centaurium calycosum
　　Swertia albomarginata - Elkweed
　　Swertia radiata
111. APOCYNACEAE — Dogbane Family
　　Apocynum cannabinum - Dogbane
112. ASCLEPIADACEAE — Milkweed Family
　　Ascelpias asperula - Antelope Horns
　　Ascelpias engelmanniana - Rusby Milkweed
　　Ascelpias speciosa
　　Ascelpias subverticillata - Poison Milkweed
　　Ascelpias tuberosa - Butterflyweed
113. CONVOLVULACEAE — Morning-glory Family
　　Convolvulus arvensis - Field Bindweed
　　Convolvulus incanus - Field Bindweed
114. POLEMONIACEAE — Phlox Family
　　Eriastrum diffusum
　　Eriastrum eremicum
　　Gilia aggregata - Skyrocket
　　Gilia multiflora
　　Linanthastrum nuttalli
　　Linanthus aureus
　　Microsteris gracilis
　　Phlox longifolia
　　Phlox woodhousei
　　Polemonium foliosissimum - Jacob's Ladder
115. HYDROPHYLLACEAE — Waterleaf Family
　　Eriodictyon angustifolium - Yerba Santa
　　Hesperochiron pumilus
　　Hydrophyllum occidentale - Waterleaf
　　Phacelia magellanica - Phacelia
　　Phacelia palmeri

116. BORAGINACEAE — Borage Family
Amsinckia tessellata - Fiddleneck
Cryptantha pterocarya
Hackelia floribunda
Lithospermum incisum - Puccoon
Lithospermum multiflorum
Macromeria viridiflora
Mertensia macdougalli - Mountain Bluebells
Pectocarya platycarpa

117. VERBENACEAE — Vervain Family
Verbena ambrosifolia - Verbena
Verbena bipinnatifida
Verbena bracteata
Verbena ciliata
Verbena gooddingii
Verbena wrightii

118. LABIATAE — Mint Family
Agastache pallidiflora
Clinopodium vulgare - Wild Basil
Hedeoma drummondi - Mock Pennyroyal
Hedeoma oblongifolium
Marrubium vulgare - Horehound
Mentha arvensis - Field-mint
Mentha spicata - Spearmint
Moldavica parviflora - Dragonhead
Monarda menthaefolia - Bee Balm
Prunella vulgaris - Self-heal
Salvia dorrii - Desert Sage
Stachys palustris

119. SOLANACEAE — Potato Family
Datura meteloides - Sacred Datura
Lycium pallidum - Wolfberry
Nicotiana attenuata - Tobacco
Solanum americanum
Solanum douglasii
Solanum elaeagnifolium - Horse Nettle
Solanum triflorum
Solanum xantii - Purple Nightshade

120. SCROPHULARIACEAE — Figwort Family
    Antirrhinum nuttallianum - Snapdragon
    Castilleja austromontana
    Castilleja chromosa - Indian Paintbrush
    Castilleja linariaefolia - Indian Paintbrush
    Cordylanthus parviflorus - Birdbeak
    Mimulus cardinalis - Crimson Monkey Flower
    Mimulus guttatus - Yellow Monkey Flower
    Mimulus rubellus
    Orthocarpus purpureo-albus - Owl Clover
    Pedicularis centranthera - Wood Betony
    Penstemon barbatus - Scarlet Beardtongue, Penstemon
    Penstemon bridgesii - Bridge's Beardtongue, Penstemon
    Penstemon eatonii - Eaton's Beardtongue, Penstemon
    Penstemon linarioides - Penstemon
    Penstemon nudiflorus
    Penstemon pachyphyllus var. *congesta* - Thick-leaf
                         Beardtongue, Penstemon
    Penstemon palmeri - Penstemon
    Penstemon pseudospectabilis - Desert Beardtongue,
                         Penstemon
    Penstemon virgatus - Penstemon
    Scrophularia parviflora - Figwort
    Verbascum thapsus - Common Mullein
    Veronica anagallis-aquatica - Water Speedwell
    Veronica persica - Speedwell

121. BIGNONIACEAE — Bignonia Family
    Chilopsis linearis - Desert Willow

122. MARTYNIACEAE — Unicorn Plant Family
    Proboscidea parviflora - Devil's Claw

123. OROBANCHACEAE — Broomrape Family
    Orobanche fasciculata - Broomrape

126. PLANTAGINACEAE — Plantain Family
    Plantago lanceolata - Buckhorn Plantain
    Plantago major - Common Plantain
    Plantago purshii - Indian Wheat

127. RUBIACEAE — Madder Family
    Galium aparine - Goosegrass Bedstraw
    Galium stellatum
    Galium triflorum - Bedstraw

Galium wrightii - Bedstraw
Houstonia wrightii
Kelloggia galioides

128. CAPRIFOLIACEAE — Honeysuckle Family
Lonicera arizonica - Honeysuckle
Sambucus glauca - Elderberry
Sambucus mexicana - Mexican Elder
Symphoricarpos parishii - Snowberry
Symphoricarpos rotundifolius - Snowberry

129. VALERIANACEAE — Valerian Family
Valeriana acutiloba
Valeriana arizonica
Valeriana edulis

130. CUCURBITACEAE — Gourd Family
Cucurbita foetidissima - Buffalo Gourd
Marah gilensis - Wild Cucumber

131. CAMPANULACEAE — Bellflower Family
Campanula parryi - Bellflower
Lobelia cardinalis - Cardinal Flower
Triodanis perfoliata - Venus Looking Glass

132. COMPOSITAE — Sunflower Family
Achilla lanulosa - Yarrow
Ambrosia psilostachya - Ragweed
Anaphalis margaritacea - Pearl Everlasting
Antennaria marginata - Pussytoes
Antennaria parvifolia
Artemisia ludoviciana - Louisiana Sagebrush
Aster adscendens - Aster
Aster arenosus
Aster bigelovii - Bigelow Aster
Aster cichoriaceus - Aster
Aster hesperius
Aster tephrodes - Aster
Baccharis emoryi - Seep Willow
Baccharis glutinosa - Seep Willow
Baileya multiradiata - Desert Marigold
Bidens tenuisecta - Spanish Needles
Brickellia californica
Brickellia floribunda

Brickellia grandifloria - Brickellia
Brickellia scabra
Chrysopsis foliosa - Golden Aster
Chrysopsis fulcrata - Golden Aster
Chrysopsis villosa - Golden Aster
Cirsium arizonicum - Arizona Thistle
Cirsium neomexicanum - New Mexico thistle
Cirsium pulchellum - Thistle
Cirsium vulgare
Conyza canadensis - Horseweed
Dyssodia acerosa
Erigeron bellidiastrum - Fleabane
Erigeron concinnus
Erigeron divergens
Erigeron eatonii
Erigeron flagellaris
Erigeron formosissimus
Erigeron macranthus - Fleabane
Erigeron nudiflorus - Daisy
Erigeron oreophilus
Erigeron pringlei
Erigeron superbus
Eupatorium herbaceum
Gaillardia pinnatifida
Gutierrezia sarothrae - Snakeweed
Haplopappus gracilis
Haplopappus ravenii
Helianthella quinquenervis - Helianthella
Helianthus annuus - Sunflower
Hieracium fendleri
Hymenopappus lugens
Hymenothrix loomisii
Hymenoxys acaulis
Hymenoxys cooperi
Lactuca graminifolia
Lactuca ludoviciana
Lactuca pulchella - Blue Lettuce
Laphamia gilensis - Laphamia
Layia glandulosa
Malacothrix fendleri

Melampodium leucanthum
Microseris linearifolia
Parthenium incanum
Perezia wrightii
Pericome caudata - Taperleaf
Perityle ciliata
Rudbeckia laciniata - Cone Flower
Senecio actinella
Senecio arizonicus - Arizona Groundsel
Senecio longilobus
Senecio macdougalii
Senecio multilobatus
Senecio neomexicanus
Senecio quercetorum - Groundsel
Senecio wootonii - Groundsel
Solidago missouriensis - Goldenrod
Solidago sparsiflora - Goldenrod
Solidago wrightii
Sonchus asper - Sow Thistle
Stephanomeria pauciflora - Wire Lettuce
Stephanomeria tenuifolia - Wire Lettuce
Taraxacum laevigatum - Dandelion
Taraxacum officinale - Dandelion
Townsendia incana - Easter Daisy
Tragopogon dubius - Goatsbeard
Verbesina encelioides - Crown Beard
Xanthium strumarium - Cocklebur

OAK CREEK AND WEST FORK
FISH CHECKLIST

Names conform to W.L. Minkley, *Fishes of Arizona*, Arizona Game and Fish Dept. 1973.

Key: N - Native; S - Stocked regularly; E - Other exotics.

SALMONIDAE
Rainbow Trout - *Salmo gairdneri* S
Brown Trout - *Salmo trutta* S
Arizona Trout - *Salmo apache* E
Gila Trout - *Salmo gilae* N
(Known only from historic records)

CYPRINIDAE
Carp - *Cyprinus carpio* E
Colorado Chub - *Gila robusta* N
Speckled Dace - *Rhinichthys osculus* N
Colorado Squawfish - *Ptychocheilus lucius* N
(Known only from historic records)

Spike Dace - *Meda fulgida* N
Fathead Minnow - *Pimephales promelas* E
Red Shiner - *Notropis lutrensis* E

CATOSTOMIDAE
Gila Sucker - *Catostomus insignis* N
Gila Mountain-sucker - *Pantosteus clarki* N

ICTALURIDAE
Channel Catfish - *Ictalurus punctatus* E
Yellow Bullhead - *Ictalurus natalis* E
Black Bullhead - *Ictalurus melas* E
Flathead Catfish - *Pilodictis olivaris* E

POECILIIDAE
Mosquito Fish - *Gambusia affinis* E

CENTRARCHIDAE
Largemouth Bass - *Micropterus salmoides* E
Smallmouth Bass - *Micropterus dolomieui* E
Green Sunfish - *Chaenobryttus cyanellus* E
Bluegill - *Lepomis macrochirus* E
Rockbass - *Ambloplites rupestris* E

OAK CREEK CANYON-RED ROCK COUNTRY
AMPHIBIAN AND REPTILE CHECKLIST

Names conform with Dowling, H.G. 1974, *Yearbook of Herpetology*, HISS: American Museum of Natural History, New York.

Key

Status	Habitat Preference
C - Common	1 - Riparian/Rain pools
U - Uncommon	2 - Ponderosa Pine-Fir
R - Rare	3 - Woodland
E - Exotic	4 - Chaparral
	5 - Desert-Grassland

AMBYSTOMIDAE
Tiger Salamander - *Ambystoma tigrinum* **C1**
PELOBATIDAE
Hammond's Spadefoot - *Scaphiopus hammondi* **U1**
BUFONIDAE
Woodhouse's Toad - *Bufo woodhousei* **C1,3**
Southwestern Toad - *Bufo microscaphus* **U1**
(West Fork only)
Red-spotted Toad - *Bufo punctatus* **U1,3**
HYLIDAE
Canyon Treefrog - *Hyla arenicolor* **U1**
Arizona Treefrog - *Hyla wrightorum* **U2**
RANIDAE
Leopard Frog - *Rana pipiens* **C1**
TESTUDINIDAE
Sonoran Mud Turtle - *Kinosternon sonoriense* **U1**
Western Box Turtle - *Terrapene ornata* **E1**
(One was found near Mayhew's Lodge. This is probably an escaped pet.)
IGUANIDAE
Texas Earless Lizard - *Cophosaurus (= Holbrooki) texanus* **C3,4,5**
Collared Lizard - *Crotaphytus collaris* **C4; U5**
Clark's Spiny Lizard - *Sceloporus clarki* **U3,4,5**
Eastern Fence Lizard - *Sceloporus undulatus* **C2,3,5; R1**

Side-blotched Lizard - *Uta stansburiana* **C4,5**
Tree Lizard - *Urosaurus ornatus* **C1; U5**
Short-horned Lizard - *Phrynosoma douglassi* **U2,3; C4**
XANTUSIIDAE
Desert Night Lizard - *Xantusia vigilis* **R2**
SCINIDAE
Many-lined Skink - *Eumeces multivirgatus* **U2,3**
Sonoran Skink - *Eumeces obsoletus* **U4**
TEIIDAE
Desert-Grassland Whiptail - *Cnemidophorus uniparens* **R4,5**
Plateau Whiptail - *Cnemidophorus velox* **U4; C3; U1**
Western Whiptail - *Cnemidophorus tigris* **C3,4**
ANGUIDAE
Arizona Alligator Lizard - *Gerrhonotus kingii* **R2; U3,4**
COLUBRIDAE
Ringneck Snake - *Diadophis punctatus* **R1**
Striped Whipsnake - *Masticophis taeniatus* **U1,3,5; C4**
Western Patch-nose Snake - *Salvadora hexalepis* **U2,3,5**
Gopher Snake - *Pituophis melanoleucus* **C2,3,5; U4**
Sonora Mountain Kingsnake - *Lampropeltis pyromelana* **U2,3,4**
Narrow-headed Garter Snake - *Thamnophis rufipunctatus* **U1**
Western Garter Snake - *Thamnophis elegans* **C1,2,3**
Night Snake - *Hypsiglena torquata* **R3,4,5**
Sonora Lyre Snake - *Trimorphodon lambda* **R2,3,4,5**
VIPERIDAE
Western Diamondback Rattlesnake - *Crotalus atrox* **R1,3; U4,5**
Western Rattlesnake - *Crotalus viridis* **U3,4,5**
Black-tailed Rattlesnake - *Crotalus molossus* **U1,3,4,5**

OAK CREEK CANYON-RED ROCK COUNTRY
BIRD CHECKLIST

Names conform with the *A.O.U. Checklist of North American Birds*, 5th ed., 1957, and 32nd Supplement. Auk 90: 411-419, 1973.

Key

Abundance	Status	Habitat Preference
C - Common	P - Permanent Resident	1 - Riparian/Pond
U - Uncommon	S - Summer Resident	2 - Ponderosa Pine-Fir
R - Rare	W - Winter Resident	3 - Woodland
I - Irregular	M - Migrant Only	4 - Chaparral
H - Hypothetical		5 - Desert Grassland

ARDEIDAE
Great Blue Heron - *Ardea herodias* **R** P1
ANATIDAE
Canada Goose - *Branta canadensis* **U** M1
Green-winged Teal - *Anas carolinensis* **C** M1
Blue-winged Teal - *Anas discor* **U** M1
Redhead - *Aythya americana* **U** M1
Ring-necked Duck - *Aythya collaris* **U** M1
Common Merganser - *Mergus merganser* **U** M1
CATHARTIDAE
Turkey Vulture - *Cathartes aura* **C** S1,3,5
ACCIPITRIDAE
Goshawk - *Accipiter gentilis* **H** P2
Sharp-shinned Hawk - *Accipiter striatus* **U** P2; **C** M
Cooper's Hawk - *Accipiter cooperii* **U** P1; **C** M
Red-tailed Hawk - *Buteo jamaicensis* **C** P1,2,3,4,5
Ferruginous Hawk - *Buteo regalis* **U** W3
Golden Eagle - *Aquila chrysaetos* **U** P2,3,4,5
Bald Eagle - *Haliaeetus leucocephalus* **U** W1
FALCONIDAE
Pigeon Hawk - *Falco columbarius* **R** W3,5
Sparrow Hawk - *Falco sparverius* **U** P1,2,3,4,5

PHASIANIDAE
   Gambel's Quail - *Lophortyx gambelii* U P3,4,5
MELEAGRIDIDAE
   Turkey - *Meleagris gallopavo* U P2; C W in canyons
RECURVIROSTRIDAE
   American Avocet - *Recurvirostra americana* R M
COLUMBIDAE
   Band-tailed Pigeon - *Columba fasciata* C S2,3
   Rock Dove - *Columba livia* C P **Sedona**
   Mourning Dove - *Zenidura macroura* C S1,3,4,5
CUCULIDAE
   Yellow-billed Cuckoo - *Coccyzus americanus* H S1
   Roadrunner - *Geococcyx californianus* R P3,5
STRIGIDAE
   Screech Owl - *Otus asio* R P3
   Flammulated Owl - *Otus flammeolus* U S2
   Great Horned Owl - *Bubo virginianus* U P1,2
   Pgymy Owl - *Glaucidium gnoma* U P2
   Elf Owl - *Macrathene whitneyi* R P1
   Saw-whet Owl - *Aegolius acadicus* U P2
CAPRIMULGIDAE
   Common Nighthawk - *Chordeiles minor* U S1,2,3,5
APODIDAE
   White-throated Swift - *Aeronautes saxatalis* C S **(cliffs)**
TROCHILIDAE
   Black-chinned Hummingbird - *Archilochus
      alexandri* C S1,3
   Broad-tailed Hummingbird - *Selasphorus
      platycercus* C S2
   Rufous Hummingbird - *Selasphorus rufus* C M
   Calliope Hummingbird - *Stellula callilope* R M2
   Rivoli's Hummingbird - *Eugenes fulgens* R S1
   Blue-throated Hummingbird - *Lampornis
      clemenciae* I S1
ALCEDINIDAE
   Belted Kingfisher - *Megaceryle alcyon* U S1
PICIDAE
   Red-shafted Flicker - *Colaptes auratus* C P1,2
   Gila Woodpecker - *Centurus uropygialis* U P1

Acorn Woodpecker - *Melanerpes formicivorus* U P1,2,3
Lewis' Woodpecker - *Asyndesmus lewis* R S1,2,3
Yellow-bellied Sapsucker - *Sphyrapicus varius* U P1,2
Williamson's Sapsucker - *Sphyrapicus
   throideus* U W2; U M
Hairy Woodpecker - *Dendrocopos villosus* C P1,2
Downy Woodpecker - *Dendrocopos pubescens* R P1,2
Ladder-backed Woodpecker - *Dendrocopos
   scalaris* C P1

TYRANNIDAE
Western Kingbird - *Tyrannus verticalis* C S1
Cassin's Kingbird - *Tyrannus vociferans* C S1
Wied's Crested Flycatcher - *Myiarchus tryannulus* U S1
Ash-throated Flycatcher - *Myiarchus cinerascens* U S1,2,3
Black Phoebe - *Sayornis nigricans* C S1; R W
Say's Phoebe - *Sayornis saya* C S1,2,3
Willow Flycatcher - *Empidonax traillii* U M
Hammond's Flycatcher - *Empidonax hammondii* U M2
Gray Flycatcher - *Empidonax wrightii* U S3
Western Flycatcher - *Empidonax difficilis* U S
Coues' Flycatcher - *Contopus pertinax* R S2
Vermillion Flycatcher - *Pyrocephalus rubinus* H S1

ALAUDIDAE
Horned Lark - *Eremophila alpestris* C P3,4,5

HIRUNDINIDAE
Violet-green Swallow - *Tachycineta thalassina* C S1,2
Rough-winged Swallow - *Stelgidopteryx ruficollis* C S1,3
Cliff Swallow - *Petrochelidon pyrrhonota* I S1

CORVIDAE
Steller's Jay - *Cyanocitta stelleri* C P1,2
Scrub Jay - *Aphelocoma coerulescens* C P3,4
Mexican Jay - *Aphelocoma ultramarina* H
Common Crow - *Corvus brachyrhynchos* U P2
Common Raven - *Corvus corax* C P2,3,4,5
Pinyon Jay - *Gymnorhinus cyanocephala* C P2,3

PARIDAE
Mountain Chickadee - *Parus gambeli* C P2
Plain Titmouse - *Parus inornatus* C P1,3,4
Bridled Titmouse - *Parus wollweberi* C P1

Common Bushtit - *Psaltriparus minimus* C P3,4

SITTIDAE
White-breasted Nuthatch - *Sitta carolinensis* C P1,2
Red-breasted Nuthatch - *Sitta canadensis* I W
Pygmy Nuthatch - *Sitta pygmaea* U P2

CERTHIIDAE
Brown Creeper - *Certhia familiaris* U P2

CINCLIDAE
Dipper - *Cinclus mexicanus* U P1

TROGLODYTIDAE
House Wren - *Troglodytes aedon* C S1,2
Winter Wren - *Troglodytes troglodytes* U W1,2
Bewick's Wren - *Thryomanes bewickii* C S1,3
Canyon Wren - *Catherpes mexicanus* C P (cliffs)
Rock Wren - *Salpinctes obsoletus* C P3,4

MIMIDAE
Mockingbird - *Mimus polyglottos* C S1, U S5
Crissal Thrasher - *Toxostoma dorsale* U P4,5
Sage Thrasher - *Oreoscoptes montanus* U S3,4,5

TURDIDAE
Robin - *Turdus migratorius* C S1,2; R W
Hermit Thrush - *Hylocichla guttata* C S1,2; R W
Swainson's Thrush - *Catharus ustulata* I M
Western Bluebird - *Sialia mexicana* C S2,3 U W3,4,5
Mountain Bluebird - *Sialia currucoides* C S2 above Mogollon
                                                    Rim
Townsend's Solitaire - *Myadestes townsendi* U P1,2

SYLVIIDAE
Blue-gray Gnatcatcher - *Polioptila caerulea* U S1,3
Golden-crowned Kinglet - *Regulus satrapa* R W
Ruby-crowned Kinglet - *Regulus calendula* U P2

MOTACILLIDAE
Water Pipit - *Anthus spinoletta* U M

BOMBYCILLIDAE
Cedar Waxwing - *Bombycilla cedrorum* R M

PTILOGONATIDAE
Phainopepla - *Phainopepla nitens* U but Irregular

LANIIDAE
Loggerhead Shrike - *Lanius ludovicianus* C S3,5

STURNIDAE
Starling - *Sturnus vulgaris* C P1,2
VIREONIDAE
Bell's Vireo - *Vireo bellii* C S1,3
Gray Vireo - *Vireo vicinior* U S3
Solitary Vireo - *Vireo solitarius* C S1,2
Warbling Vireo - *Vireo gilvus* C S1,2
PARULIDAE
Orange-crowned Warbler - *Vermivora celata* U S4
Nashville Warbler - *Vermivora ruficapilla* U M
Virginia's Warbler - *Vermivora virginiae* U S
Lucy's Warbler - *Vermivora luciae* U S1
Olive Warbler - *Peucedramus taeniatus* seen in Loy Canyon
Jan. 1976
Yellow Warbler - *Dendroica petechia* C S1
Audubon's Warbler - *Dendroica coronata* C S2
Black-throated Gray Warbler - *Dendroica nigrescens* C S3
Townsend's Warbler - *Dendroica townsendi* C M2
Hermit Warbler - *Dendroica occidentalis* U M2
Grace's Warbler - *Denroica graciae* C S2; U S3
MacGillivray's Warbler - *Oporonis tolmiei* U 1,2,4
Yellowthroat - *Geothlypis trichas* R S1
Yellow-breasted Chat - *Icteria virens* C S1
Red-faced Warbler - *Cardellina rubrifrons* U S1,2
Wilson's Warbler - *Wilsonia pusilla* C M
Painted Redstart - *Setophaga picta* U S1
American Redstart - *Setophaga ruticilla* R S1
PLOCEIDAE
House Sparrow - *Passer domesticus* U P1
ICTERUDAE
Western Meadowlark - *Sturnella neglecta* U S1,5
Red-winged Blackbird - *Agelaius phoeniniceus* U S1
Hooded Oriole - *Icterus cucullatus* U S1
Scott's Oriole - *Icterus parisorum* U S3,5
Bullock's Oriole - *Icterus galbula* U S1
Brewer's Blackbird - *Euphagus cyanocephalus* U S1,2,3
Brown-headed Cowbird - *Molothrus ater* U S1,2,3
THRAUPIDAE
Western Tanager - *Piranga ludoviciana* C S1,2

Hepatic Tanager - *Piranga flava* U S2,3
Summer Tanager - *Piranga rubra* C S1

FRINGILLIDAE
Cardinal - *Richmondena cardinalis* U P1,3,4,5
Black-headed Grosbeak - *Pheucticus melanocephalus* C S1,2
Blue Grosbeak - *Guiraca caerulea* R S1
Indigo Bunting - *Passerina cyanea* U S1
Lazuli Bunting - *Passerina amoena* U S1,4
Evening Grosbeak - *Hesperiphona vespertina* U W2
Cassin's Finch - *Carpodacus cassinii* R M2
House Finch - *Carpodacus mexicanus* C P1,2
Pine Siskin - *Spinus pinus* C P2
American Goldfinch - *Spinus tristis* R M
Lesser Goldfinch - *Spinus psaltria* C S1,2,5
Red Crossbill - *Loxia curvirostra* R P2
Green-tailed Towhee - *Chlorura chlorura* R M
Rufous-sided Towhee - *Pipilo erythrophthalmus* C S4
Brown Towhee - *Pipilo fuscus* U P3,4
Albert's Towhee - *Pipilo alberti* U S1
Lark Sparrow - *Chondestes grammacus* U 1,2,3
Rufous-Crowned Sparrow - *Aimophila ruficeps* U S4
Black-throated Sparrow - *Amphispiza bilineata* C S3,4,5
Oregon Junco - *Junco oreganus* C W1,2
Gray-headed Junco - *Junco caniceps* C P2
Chipping Sparrow - *Spizella passerina* C S1,2
Brewer's Sparrow - *Spizella breweri* C S2,3
Black-chinned Sparrow - *Spizella atrogularis* C S3,4
White-crowned Sparrow - *Zonotrichia leucophrys* C W1,5
Lincoln's Sparrow - *Melospiza lincolnii* U W
Song Sparrow - *Melospiza melodia* U S; R W

OAK CREEK CANYON-RED ROCK COUNTRY
MAMMAL CHECKLIST

Names conform with Jones, Carter, and Genoways. 1975
Revised Checklist of North American Mammals North of Mexico,
Occ. Papers, The Museum, Texas Tech Univ.

Key

Status	Habitat Preference
C - Common	1 - Riparian
U - Uncommon	2 - Ponderosa Pine-Fir
R - Rare	3 - Woodland
M - Migrant	4 - Chaparral
H - Hypothetical	5 - Desert-Grassland

SORICIDAE
  Merriam's Shrew - *Sorex merriami* **R2**
  Desert Shrew - *Notiosorex crawfordi* **R1,3,5**
VESPERTILIONIDAE*
  Little Brown Myotis - *Myotis lucifugus*
  Yuma Myotis - *Myotis yumanensis*
  Cave Myotis - *Myotis velifer*
  Long-eared Myotis - *Myotis evotis*
  Fringed Myotis - *Myotis thysanodes*
  Long-legged Myotis - *Myotis volans*
  California Myotis - *Myotis californicus*
  Small-footed Myotis - *Myotis leibii*
  Silver-haired Bat - *Lasionycteris noctivagans*
  Western Pipistrelle - *Pipistrellus hesperus*
  Big Brown Bat - *Eptesicus fuscus*
  Red Bat - *Lasiurus borealis*
  Hoary Bat - *Lasiurus cinereus*
  Townsend's Big-eared Bat - *Plecotus townsendii*
  Allen's Big-eared Bat - *Idionycteris phyllotis*
  Pallid Bat - *Antrozous pallidus*
MOLOSSIDAE*
  Brazilian Freetail Bat - *Tadarida brasiliensis*
LEPORIDAE
  Desert Cottontail - *Sylvilagus audubonii* **U3,4,5**

Black-tailed Jack Rabbit - *Lepus californicus* **C3,5; U4**

SCIURIDAE
Harris' Antelope Squirrel - *Ammospermophilus harrisii* **U3,5**
Rock Squirrel - *Spermophilus variegatus* **C2,3,4**
Golden-mantled Ground Squirrel - *Spermophilus lateralis* **C2**
Gray-Collared Chipmunk - *Eutamias cinereicollis* **U2**
Cliff Chipmunk - *Eutamias dorsalis* **C2,3,4**
Abert's Squirrel - *Sciurus aberti* **C2**
Arizona Gray Squirrel - *Sciurus arizonensis* **U1**
Red Squirrel - *Tamiasciurus hudsonicus* **U2**

GEOMYIDAE
Botta's Pocket Gopher - *Thomomys bottae* **U2**

CASTORIDAE
Beaver - *Castor canadensis* **H1**

CRICETIDAE
Western Harvest Mouse - *Reithrodontomys megalotis* **R3**
Deer Mouse - *Peromyscus maniculatus* **C1,2,3,4,5**
Brush Mouse - *Peromyscus boylii* **C2,3,4,5**
Pinyon Mouse - *Peromyscus truei* **U3**
White-throated Woodrat - *Neotoma albigula* **U3,4,5**
Stephens' Woodrat - *Neotoma stephensi* **U3**
Mexican Woodrat - *Neotoma mexicana* **U1,2,3**
Mexican Vole - *Microtus mexicanus* **U1,2**
Muskrat - *Ondatra zibethicus* **R1**

MURIDAE
House Mouse - *Mus musculus* **C dwellings**

ERETHIZONTIDAE
Porcupine - *Erethizon dorsatum* **U1,2,3**

CANIDAE
Coyote - *Canis latrans* **U2,3,5**
Gray Fox - *Urocyon cinereoargenteus* **U1; R2,3,4,5**

URSIDAE
Black Bear** - *Ursus americanus* **R1,2**

PROCYONIDAE
Raccoon - *Procyon lotor* **U1**
Coati - *Nasua nasua* **R4 Two seen in Oak Creek Canyon,**
             1962
Ringtail - *Bassariscus astutus* **U1**

MUSTELIDAE
  Long-tail Weasel - *Mustela frenata* **R2**
  Badger - *Taxidea taxus* **R3**
  Spotted Skunk - *Spilogale gracilis* **U1,3,4,5**
  Striped Skunk - *Mephitis mephitis* **C1,2,3,4,5**
FELIDAE
  Mountain Lion** - *Felis concolor* **R1,2,3,4**
  Bobcat - *Lynx rufus* **R1,2,3,4**
TAYASSUIDAE
  Collared Peccary** - *Dicotyles tajacu* **U3,4**
CERVIDAE
  Wapiti** - *Cervus canadensis* **R2,3**
  Mule Deer - *Odocoileus hemionus* **U2,3,4,5**
  White-tailed Deer - *Odocoileus virginianus* **U2,3,4,5**

*   Abundance and migratory status unknown
** Almost totally restricted to the more remote areas and/or rim country

INDEX

Numbers in *italics* indicate pages on which illustrations occur.
For scientific names of the plants and animals see the Checklists.

Notes

Notes

Notes

Notes

Notes

Notes